Conflict Ministry in the Church

Larry L. McSwain
and
William C. Treadwell, Jr.

The Ministerial Association
General Conference of Seventh-day Adventists
Silver Spring, MD 20904

Funding for this series has been provided by
J. A. Thomas & Associates, Inc.
Atlanta, Georgia

The Scripture quotations in this publication are from the Revised Standard Version of the Bible, copyrighted 1946, 1952, © 1971, 1973 by the National Council of the Churches of Christ in the U.S.A., and are used by permission.

© 1997 Ministerial Association

Published by Ministerial Association
General Conference of Seventh-day Adventists
12501 Old Columbia Pike
Silver Spring, Maryland 20904-6600

This book was originally published by Broadman Publishing House under the same title in 1981. All copy has been reset and repaginated.

*Printed in the U.S.A. by Review and Herald Graphics
Hagerstown, Maryland 21740*

Contents

          Earn Continuing Education Credit 4
          Acknowledgement 5
          Tables and Figures 6
          Preface 7

Chapter 1   Panorama: The Conflict Ministry Process 11

Chapter 2   Stress: The Root of Conflict 37

Chapter 3   Interpersonal Conflict: Everyone Needs
                  a Referee Occasionally 59

Chapter 4   Congregational Fights: Organizational
                  and Community Conflicts 83

Chapter 5   Styles and Resources for Conflict Ministry 117

          Conclusions: Will Conflict Never End? 133
          Bibliography 137
          CEU Registration Request 143

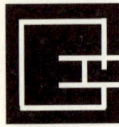

The Continuing Education Unit •

Earn Continuing Education Credit*

Each chapter of this book concludes with an "Assignment" section prepared by Ministerial Continuing Education. If you read all chapters of this volume and faithfully perform all of the prescribed exercises, you qualify for two Continuing Education Units (CEUs) which fulfill the annual continuing education requirement for Seventh-day Adventist ministers. Complete the CEU Registration Request on page 137.

> *Never think that you have learned enough, and that you may now relax yours efforts. The cultivated mind is the measure of a man. Your education should continue during your lifetime; every day you should be learning, and putting to practical use the knowledge gained.*
> —Ellen G. White,
> Testimonies for the Church, *vol. 4, p. 561.*

*CEUs are non-academic credit and cannot be applied to a degree.

Acknowledgments

Appreciation is expressed to the following publishers for their permission to quote from selected literature:

Journal of Psychosomatic Research, Volume 11, Thomas H. Holmes and Richard H. Rahe, "The Social Readjustment Rating Scale," 1967, Pergamon Press, Ltd.

From *Is There Hope for the City?* by Donald W. Shriver, Jr. and Karl A. Ostrom (Biblical Perspectives on Current Issues, Howard Clark Kee, General Editor). Copyright © 1977 The Westminster Press. Used by permission.

Caring Enough to Confront by David Augsburger. © Copyright revised edition 1980 by Harold Press, used by permission of G/L Publications, Ventura, CA 93003.

From *Interpersonal Conflict Resolution*, by Alan L. Filley. Copyright © 1975, Scott, Foresman and Company. Used by permission.

From *Living with Stress*, by Nancy E. Gross. © Copyrighted by Nancy E. Gross, 1958. Used by permission.

From *New Ways of Managing Conflict* by Rensis and Jane Gibson Likert. © Copyrighted by McGraw-Hill Book Company, 1976. Used by permission.

Tables and Figures

Figure 1-1 Sources of Conflict .... p. 17
Figure 1-2 The Conflict Process .... p. 18
Figure 1-3 The Conflict Ministry Process .... pp. 20-21
Figure 1-4 Context for Conflict .... p. 24
Figure 1-5 Forms of Engagement .... p. 29
Figure 2-1 Social Readjustment Rating Scale .... p. 41
Figure 3-1 Growth Toward Balance Between Trust
                and Exposure .... p. 66
Figure 4-1 Flow of Preparation in Decision-Making
                Process .... p. 95
Figure 4-2 Elements of Decision Making .... p. 97
Figure 4-3 Growth for People of God .... p. 98
Figure 4-4 Conclusion of Decision Making .... p. 99
Figure 4-5 Cycles of Conflict Ministry .... p. 100
Figure 5-1 Relation Between Conflict Style and
                Source of Conflict .... p. 124

Preface

Monday is often the most difficult day of the week for a Christian who is committed to ministry through the church. It is the day many want to resign after a difficult Sunday.

Elizabeth Daily is the volunteer coordinator of the Youth Division of the Sunday School of Immanuel Church. One Monday in mid-July of last year she appeared at the church office at 10:00 a.m. seeking the pastor. He was in his study reviewing the attendance and record of giving from the day before. She entered and blurted, "Reverend Anthony, I know you will hate me for saying this, but I just can't wait until new teachers are selected in October. This Youth Division is driving me crazy. Bobby Richardson is impossible to control, and I can't take it any longer. We have to make some changes or I must resign."

"I know you are frustrated," responded James Anthony, her minister of three years. "And I will not hate you for coming to share your frustrations with me. Let's see how we can work out the situation."

James Anthony met her needs by listening sympathetically and offering concrete suggestions for resolving a team problem in the Youth Division. What Elizabeth did not know, however, was the extent of her pastor's frustration. It was Monday for him, too. The attendance had been poor the previous day, and the offerings were lower than any Sunday during his pastorate. Last month three of the deacons had voiced their opposition to his leadership and threatened to move to another church if the church did not begin to show greater numerical growth. It seemed to him that his preaching was as effective when directed to the walls of the sanctuary as when he spoke to the people. Elizabeth Daily's problems simply added to his sense of stress. He went home for lunch that day and shared with his wife Christine his deep anxiety. "This is the second church I have served where it seems we have nothing but problems," he said. "Maybe I ought to consider the possibility that the pastorate is not where God wants me."

Monday is a day for such thoughts. After the intense activity of the church on Sunday, church staff members and lay persons often reflect upon the successes and failures of the previous day. When Sunday has been a day of victory and celebration, Monday thoughts turn to questions of how to perpetuate that spirit. When it has been a day of apathy and conflict, the word *resignation* almost always finds its way into Monday thoughts. *Surprise* is perhaps the most characteristic word to describe our feeling about conflict in the church. Somehow we expect more or better of the people of God. The first reaction to some new revelation of a broken marriage, a ruptured fellowship, or a dismissed pastor is usually denial. "It just isn't so," we say. Even when we accept the reality of conflict, we often do so with heavy feelings of guilt: "What have we done to merit this?" Then the guilt turns to anger and hostility. These feelings are what "dark" Mondays are all about.

This is a book to be read on those "dark" Mondays when you feel like changing churches, resigning your Sunday School class, or leaving the pastoral ministry. We have written this guide to help you analyze the conflicts, disagreements, and tensions which arise in all churches. We believe a better understanding of how conflict works and what can be done about it will assist you to minister more effectively in your church. We will offer only one rule to you our reader: "Never resign on Monday!" Read this book instead.

The goal of this book is to provide you a practical guide for dealing with conflict in the church. Much has been written to offer business personnel, teachers, and community leaders help in managing conflict in their vocations. We have drawn from these human relations sources and combined them with insights from Scripture and the experiences of other Christian leaders to offer a resource specifically for churches. Our thesis is that conflict situations offer the Christian an opportunity to minister to others as a reconciling servant of Jesus Christ. We pray that as you read this book you can draw resources from it to meet more effectively the needs of others in the midst of seemingly impossible situations.

We are sure the church of Jesus Christ has the potential to be a caring, forgiving, peaceful expression of the presence of God in its midst. There is a divine quality to be found wherever God's people assemble themselves for worship and service (Matt. 18:20).

Sometimes that divine quality is to be found in the midst of a group of folks who gather in a brick building at the corner of Fifth and Main, or within a white clapboard building in the open countryside. For others, it is found in an apartment Bible study in a high rise containing 300 units of urban cubicles. The apostle Paul describes this human community of believers as an "earthen vessel" (2 Cor. 4:7). By this he meant the church is a *human* community which has all the characteristics of other human groups. As a human community the

PREFACE

church struggles to live with Christ as its center. But it is never perfect, never fully divine. This serves, as Paul says, "to show that the transcendent power belongs to God and not to us" (2 Cor. 4:7).

This is a book for all of the "earthen vessels," for the only churches we can write about are communities of disciples who gather in places week by week to learn of Jesus. They live with the daily realities of misunderstanding, differences, intrapersonal struggles, interpersonal warfare, organizational blowups, and community controversies which are a part of life. It is our hope that pastors, lay leaders, and denominational leaders may discover in these pages a useful guide to the myriad ways in which churches can minister more effectively to persons in conflict.

We do not wish to ignore the more pleasant aspects of church life by focusing upon what is often unpleasant. Rather, we choose to examine in detail what is frequently denied by church leaders.

This book centers upon one of the dimensions of reality, conflict. Some will not want to read it for the very word *conflict* conjures in the imagination painful memories of arguments, hurt feelings, violences, and hatred. "Why deal with such negative matters?" we say to ourselves. "Let's think and talk of peace, freedom, love, and reconciliation!"

Is not the memory selective about the events of the past? Think back through your most thrilling moments of peace, freedom, love, and reconciliation. Did they not occur as the result of successfully dealing with a problem, difficulty, or conflict? We hope you will read this book because we believe that the results of healthy conflict are positive, productive, and potentially joyful. We believe persons can and should *learn* how to deal with life's conflicts in such a way as to experience wholeness and peace.

Reading a book is very much like taking a journey. One needs a map to know where one is going. We hope this book can guide you in serving Jesus Christ more effectively as a minister with persons in conflict. We cannot promise an easy journey.

We have tried to write the book so that each chapter builds upon the first, which sets forth a process of conflict ministry. While each chapter can be read independently, we encourage you to begin with the process, which may then be applied to the subsequent emphases on conflict in intrapersonal, interpersonal, and intergroup settings.

No one writes a book without struggle. When two persons write one, the struggle can become conflict. We have tried to practice the insights recorded here by making this a covenant pilgrimage. We began with an agreement to talk and work together until either the words were forged into pages or we could go no further.

The process was not always easy. One of us, primarily an academician, worked for precision, consistency with published research, and theoretical congruence. The other of us, primarily an experienced practitioner in the art of conflict ministry, sought clarity of language, consistency with life experience, and usefulness for today's laity. Others must judge whether we have sufficiently blended the two into a useful form.

Fellow pilgrims have enriched our journey together, to whom we must express appreciation. First, we thank those clergy whose written experiences provided many of the case studies used to illustrate our process. Most were Doctor of Ministry students whose conflict settings must remain anonymous.

Our families have supported us in more ways than we can describe. Both our wives, Sue and Lou, have been a part of the conflicts in which we live and have ministered to us and with us. And our children were understanding and loving when we were preoccupied with "completing another chapter."

The institutions which have supported us financially, The Southern Baptist Theological Seminary, the Crescent Hill Baptist Church, Louisville Kentucky, and the Faith Baptist Church, Georgetown, Kentucky, have provided environments for practicing the book as well as free time for reflection and writing. Most of the theoretical material was developed during a sabbatical leave granted Larry L. McSwain by the trustees of The Southern Baptist Theological Seminary. He is most grateful for this form of institutional support.

Finally, we acknowledge the gifts of friendship by those who read and reacted to multiple drafts of the final product: D. Glenn Saul, Golden Gate Baptist Theological Seminary; G. Willis Bennett, Fred Andrea, James McDowell, Rudee Boan, and Jan Hix of The Southern Baptist Theological Seminary; and Bruce Grubbes of The Sunday School Board of the Southern Baptist Convention. Our special thanks go to Alicia Gardner, Carol Gates, and Janet Forrest for their supervision of the typing, and to Mrs. Kathy Melton, Mrs. Jan McDowell, Mrs. Carolyn Helms, and Mrs. Louise Limehouse for their typing of the drafts of the manuscript.

Chapter 1

Panorama: The Conflict Ministry Process

Every beginning is pregnant with promise. Marriages begin with the promises of love and fidelity. Birth inaugurates the potential for human growth and achievement. Churches organize to live out a dream of community under the leadership of God's spirit.

However promises get broken, and dreams are easily shattered. All of us have experienced the pain of broken marriage covenants, children who fail to fulfill their potential, and Christian congregations in which there is little fellowship. Every promise can become no more than a forgotten ideal.

Life is the effort of trying to make our promises come true. Where the vision of promise diminishes, despair develops in the human heart. If a promise dies, life can become hellish.

Conflict ministry is a process for keeping alive the hope of fulfilled promises, for this ministry requires becoming involved with people at the point of their pain, sinfulness, and meanness. It requires human interaction at the deepest level, where people" bump" into each other and find out whether they can communicate with one another and work with one another. In conflict we must learn to live with each other as though we were members of the same family. This is called *intimacy.* And intimacy is not easy. One pastor we know described the pain of a disruption in the church he serves over the issue of "spiritual gifts." Here is his description of an effort to reconcile growing conflict:

A charismatic, neo-Pentecostal element has been active in our church for approximately four years. It began with a previous pastor's wife holding prayer meetings in the parsonage and has grown considerably during these past years.

A few weeks after I arrived on the field six months ago, I was informed of this situation, as the church has not traditionally accepted this emphasis. During my visits in the community, I had the opportunity to talk with the leader of the Pentecostal group, a teacher in our young married women's class named Roberta Young. I discussed with her my stand on the subject. I tried to convince her that I had no problem with "tongues" as long as they were practiced biblically. Roberta assured me she did not try to force her beliefs on the class or teach contrary to biblical beliefs.

During the monthly deacons' meeting, I discussed this situation with the deacons. They informed me that when it had been learned by the previous pastor that the teacher of this class had Pentecostal leanings he had placed the minister of youth in the class to observe. The issue had never been brought up again. They did note, however, that the group had held weekly meetings in their homes during this time and had begun attending prayer group meetings in the local Pentecostal Church.

As the weeks passed I began to see and to hear of Roberta's serious digression from the position she had described to me. The lessons in the class became more and more a confessional time for the teacher. The lessons in our denominational literature were seldom followed. Because, she said, some members were reluctant to read in class, the Scriptures were not used to any extent except to support her position. The situation came to a head during a lesson on the Holy Spirit in which some of the Pentecostals in the class suggested that the others in the class might not be true Christians because they had not received the "second blessing" of the Spirit. Because of the confusion that resulted from this class session I asked the class to meet in my home the next evening to discuss the issues of tongues and the Holy Spirit.

The meeting was attended by most of the class members, and even a few members of the local Pentecostal Church were on hand to give support to the teacher's position. The meeting began with a prayer and a brief dialogue as to the issues involved, so we could stick with the essential questions. Following this I simply began to read chapters 12—14 in 1 Corinthians; Acts 2; and Romans 8, all of which the Pentecostals had used to support their position. I concluded with the historical background surrounding these issues. As I read, the class members would comment. Soon the position of the Pentecostals became less and less acceptable to the vast majority of the class. I noticed Roberta and her followers beginning to experience sharp intakes of breath, to shake their heads in a negative fashion, and to mutter among themselves, "That's not right!" After the reading of the Scriptures, discussion was invited. The Pentecostals deluged the conversation with unrelated Scripture which tended to confuse rather than clarify the issues involved. During most of this time, Roberta remained very quiet and would usually conclude any remark she did make with "I want you all to know how much I love you." It became obvious that even those in the class who disagreed with her stand were subject to her forceful and motherly leadership. There was a very close bond of affection toward her in the class.

After this meeting I visited both groups of members, trying to find some grounds of reconciliation. On the surface it appeared the conflict has settled down somewhat, even though rumors continued to flourish around town.

The final conflict between these two groups came last week at another class meeting. The meeting began with a good sense of fellowship, but when Roberta took the floor she spent approximately an hour and a half expounding on the virtues of the local Pentecostal Church and its beliefs. When asked by class members why she continued to teach in our church, she replied that she did not have a car to go to the Pentecostal Church. She felt it was her responsibility to lead this class to a greater knowledge of the Holy Spirit, Roberta concluded, even though she said she did not believe in the doctrines of our church because they were made by men. She concluded her remarks by stating that it appeared most of the women were "searching" for faith and suggesting it would be a good idea to bring the local Pentecostal minister's wife to the next meeting so she could answer their questions. This was promptly seconded by the associate teacher, another Pentecostal.

That evening I spent a great deal of time on the telephone talking to those who came away from this meeting feeling inferior because they did not have a "secret prayer language" or the ability to speak in "tongues." I tried to reassure these women that this had little to do with salvation and offered prayer and suggestions of readings from the Bible concerning the nature and value of "tongues."

During the next few days I visited most of those present at the meeting, trying to determine what was actually said. After evaluating the information given to me (by both sides), I decided that a more decisive course of action was called for. That Saturday the deacons and I met to discuss the issues involved, and after a lengthy discussion, it was decided that two of the deacons and I would go see Roberta Young and ask that she resign her position. We felt she disagreed with the principles on which we base our faith and believed we were "agents of Satan."

When conflict like this erupts in a church fellowship, the hope of what the church can be as a caring fellowship fades. "Why" becomes our first question. The promise of Jesus' "Peace I leave with you" (John 14:27) seems so distant on such occasions. We must be reminded constantly that His way of peace is costly. It cannot be won through rational argument alone, as important as rationality is. It requires more than negotiation and good management skills. There is a second part to the promise of John 14:27, "Not as the world gives do I give to you."

In any form of conflict ministry there must be the recognition that reconciling peace is a gift of God. It is not earned, but given. Meaningful ministry in settings of human fragmentation and alienation must begin with the theological understandings of conflict. Why conflict? What is its source? Can it be affirmed within the church if the peace of God is what we seek? A brief overview of a theological basis for understanding conflict will help resolve these questions.

Understanding Conflict Theologically

The reality of conflict will remain a mystery forever to those who deal with it unless there can be a common understanding of it. Conflict was not God's plan for humanity. The biblical account of creation affirms that from the very beginning of human history there was a harmony of human relationships, which was God's intention for humanity. The peace *(shalom)* for which persons and human institutions yearn was implanted in the human experience because we are created by God.

Peace is a quality which belongs ultimately to God. It is a sense of well-being within and between persons and nations and the ending of hatred and enmity between enemies.[1] A careful study of Ephesians 2:14-18; 2 Corinthians 5:17-21; and Colossians 1:19-21 clearly indicates the reality that fallen mankind is the enemy of God. God is the initiator who changes humanity through the action of Jesus Christ. By taking upon Himself on the cross the hatred of humanity and the cosmos, the enmity between God and persons could be ended. Only by becoming involved in conflict could the conflict be laid to rest.

The doctrine of creation is the foundation of any adequate understanding of how we are to have hope amid the conflicts we face. This can be seen in Jesus' approach to one of the most painful of human conflict situations, the problem of divorce. When confronted with the feuding factions of Jewish interpreters on the question, followers of Hillel and Shammai (Matt. 19:3-9),[2] He stated the purpose of God in creation. Man and woman were created with the capacities of *henosis* or one flesh—a unity of personal relationship with each other that provides the basis of meaningful sexual, emotional, and spiritual union without the loss of unique individual personalities.[3] Divorce was a concession of the Mosaic law to the reality of human failure. In the vision of creation, there could be no such reality as divorce or any other form of conflict between persons.

The doctrine of creation affirms the vision of a conflict-free existence. In the Bible's description of Adam and Eve there is the reality of the divine expectation for mankind. It is the picture of wholeness for persons, meaningful union without manipulation between the sexes, an ecological balance between humanity and nature, and perfect communion between the Creator and the created. There is freedom without limitation, sensuality without guilt, communication without distortion, and communion without fracture. To this vision of the creation Jesus called His followers. If the vision of creation were the goal for human marriage, as we have seen, why could it not also be the vision for all of life's transactions?

But the vision has been shattered. Persons living in the now of life's journeys must deal with the broken reality of a fracture between Creator and creation. As the poet Yeats declares, "Things fall apart, the center cannot hold."[4] The choice of humans in the freedom of creation resulted in a turning away from the God of the vision. Since freedom requires the potential of choice, men and women choose to reject the unity of relationship with the Creator. The consequence is the loss of the unity of creation. Life is a broken existence. So we see life like the reflections in a broken mirror—fragmented and broken because of the choices we make in violation of the Creator's vision for our lives. The doctrine of the fall is the description of human turning from the Creator to live in disobedience as a consequence of this choice. Conflict is introduced into every dimension of human reality because of human sin. Adam became a wandering alien in the land of Nod, and his child, Cain, a murderer because of this sin. The source of conflict in the world is this human sin.

The doctrine of salvation records the Creator's initiatives to restore the vision of the Garden in human experience. The covenant of Yahweh with Abraham was His call to establish a unique people who would live out the vision in a universal nation (Gen. 12:1-3). The Law of Yahweh with Moses was God's action at work in human history to reorder human relationships according to the model of creation (Ex. 20:1-17). Prophets, priests, and kings were established to become embodiments of the plan of God for a new reality based upon the eternal purpose of history. The means of the divine initiative to restore wholeness to the created order have been multiple, and each action from the Father has been met with both acceptance and rejection from His creation.

The supreme manifestation of God seeking man became realized in the incarnation of His being in Jesus of Nazareth. In Him God's ultimate initiative for His creation was revealed. The conflicts of human history were to be reconciled in a unique way.

A thorough examination of that way reveals the picture of a man who became a peacemaker within the violence, estrangement, hatred, and fracture of His Judaic setting. He sought the kingdom of God as His highest priority. In Mark 1:15 He proclaimed, "The time is fulfilled, and the kingdom of God is at hand." Both a present fact and a future reality are found here. Jesus was the gift of the kingdom and the bearer of the kingdom. He lived in His world as though God's future promises were already here. Such a commitment thrust Him into the center of intellectual debate (Luke 20:27-40); political turmoil (Matt. 22:15-22); personal anguish (Luke 8:43-48); family misunderstanding (Mark 3:20-35); economic conflict (Luke 12:13-21); and religious ferment (Matt. 21:12-13).

Only by encountering conflict, bringing it into the light of truth, and accepting it into the totality of His being was God able to bring the wholeness of His salvation to the created order. The meaning of salvation is found in the event of Jesus the Christ. In His living, teaching, dying upon the cross, and the victorious resurrection from death the meaning of reconciliation became known. The resolution of conflict is the way of reconciliation. Only as Jesus assumed within Himself the conflicts of humanity could the conflicts of humanity become settled.[5] Thus, the way of reconciliation is the way of accepting the supreme symbol of human conflict—the cross.[6]

Thus we understand the intention of God for His church. With the resurrection of Jesus the Christ the people of God became the incarnate presence of the Son of God in human history through the indwelling of the Holy Spirit. The life, ministry, death, and resurrection of Jesus continue in the world as they are lived out in the lives of His followers. Conflict can be constructively encountered in our history as Spirit-led disciples take unto themselves the cross of their Lord (Luke 9:23). In daily obedience sharing His suffering, the contemporary ministry of the church is to become the agent of reconciliation by bearing within its community the conflicts of the world. As Jesus Christ became the great reconciler of creation, so we are called to be ministers of reconciliation (2 Cor. 5:16-20). If Jesus' supreme act of reconciliation was the obedience of death through encounter with conflict, our ministry of reconciliation must be a living encounter with conflict in all its forms.

"Such a mission seems impossible," one might well say. And it is, apart from a final theological understanding. That is the doctrine of the end or eschatology. How is it that the Christian can respond to an invitation to conflict without despair? A Christian can do this through hope in the vision of the end. God's promise to His people is that everything He set out to do in creation He will complete with the return of Jesus as Lord. The vision of creation is fulfilled in the reality of the Kingdom, heaven, and eternity. So it is that His disciples live with hope within the struggles of a fallen world. In Jesus the beginning of the end has dawned. The reconciliation that will be consummated universally at the end of time has already occurred in His acts of obedience. So we live daily with the suffering of conflict in the experience of reconciliation within our own lives. As reconciliation occurs now a foretaste of the future is experienced. We can begin to know the extent of the promise we shall inherit in resurrection to the eternal kingdom, in which the joy of creation shall again be experienced eternally.[7]

Is conflict necessary, then? Yes, because sin has made its impression upon all persons. Must it be so prevalent in the church? Yes, for the church is a community of sinners being saved by grace. It has not yet been redeemed into God's future kingdom. Must I deal with conflict as a part of my commitment to His church? Yes, for any ministry of reconciliation assumes there are people in need of reconciliation. If people refuse to recognize and deal with conflict, there can be no reconciliation.

God's intention for His followers is that they become equipped to serve Him as conflict ministers. How? That is the question the remainder of the book seeks to answer by drawing upon the insights of Scripture, management theory, sociological analyses, and psychological insights into human behavior. Let us begin by exploring together an overview of conflict and a process for responding to it with Christian insight.

The Nature of Conflict

What do we mean by conflict? The root meaning of the word is "to strike."[8] Close your eyes and imagine different kinds of conflict. What do you see? Can you see a couple "striking" each other with abusive words? Two high school football players pounding against each other as they practice blocking? A father spanking his child? Boxers in a ring punching each other's bodies? Airplanes

PANORAMA: THE CONFLICT MINISTRY PROCESS

dropping bombs behind enemy lines? Hands being raised to vote at a church business meeting? A father and son arguing over whether the son should register for the military draft?

Conflict describes those experiences of individuals and groups trying to achieve goals which are either incompatible or appear to be so. A conflict is "a situation in which two or more human beings desire goals which they perceive as being attainable by one or the other *but not by both.*"[9]

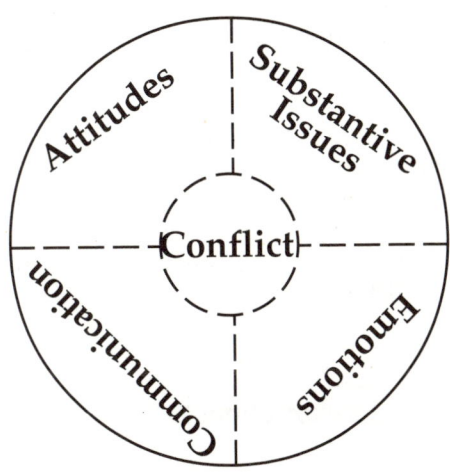

Figure 1-1: Sources of Conflict

There are four different sources of conflict which can be experienced in the church. These are illustrated in Figure 1-1. It will not be possible to isolate only one of these in real life conflict situations. For they tend to interact with each other, as indicated by the dotted lines in the diagram. In most situations of conflict, however, one primary cause of the conflict can be isolated. Determining the specific nature of the conflict will be important in providing ministry in that situation.

Attitudinal conflict emerges when individuals have differences of feelings or perspectives about persons and issues. Prejudices, stereotypes, or particular beliefs are all attitudes which people carry with them. When attitudes differ, people find themselves bumping into each other in conflictual ways.

Substantive conflict emerges when there are differences of opinion about facts, goals, ends, or means. Two groups in the church may disagree regarding the Bible's teaching on the proper mode of baptism. They have a substantive conflict.

Emotional conflict results when personal value is attached either to attitudinal or to substantive forms of conflict. Persons who have been harmed physically by a member of another race may have great difficulty in holding Christian attitudes toward any person of that race. Such a prejudice has become emotionally rigid, so that logical arguments will have little effect in changing it. Efforts to change the attitude are viewed as personal attacks.

Communicative conflict is a by-product of a breakdown in healthy, open conversation about the sources of conflict. We believe communication is the key to a reconciling ministry in each of the other forms of conflict. Poor communication heightens the hurt which can emerge from attitudinal, substantive, or emotional conflict.

Conflict is a process. Regardless of the source of a given conflict, there are stages of development through which it passes. Understanding this process is the beginning point of learning how to minister in its midst.

Figure 1-2 illustrates the process of a conflict. The elements of this process are:

Assumptions—In every conflict situation the persons involved have a set of assumptions about conflict, what to do in conflict, and how conflict should be settled.

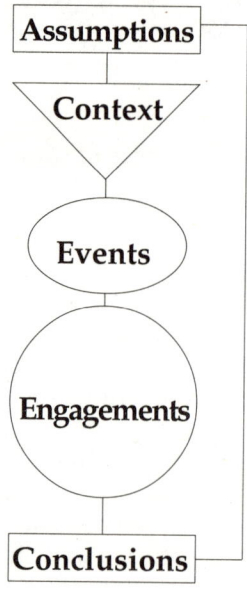

Figure 1-2: The Conflict Process

Context—There is a particular setting in which conflict occurs. Some contexts produce more conflict than others. The symbol of context in this process is triangular, for there are three aspects to any context. These are the prior experiences of those in conflict, the quality of human relationships between them, and the policies of the structures within which they function.

Events—Conflict events are those occurrences which bring to public awareness the fact of conflict. A fight may "brew" for a long time before anyone knows it is developing. When a divorce is announced, a church split occurs, or two church leaders resign in a dispute, the event symbolizing underlying conflict has taken place.

Engagements—We call the way people respond to conflict events engagement. Some persons may withdraw from conflict. Others become combative. Ministry occurs when the forms of engagement reflect the mind of Christ.

Conclusions—Every conflict must eventually end. If the conclusion to a conflict is healthy, Christian growth occurs for the parties involved. If not, additional conflict may ensue. This is indicated in Figure 1-2 with the line drawn from conclusions to assumptions. Mishandled conflict starts the cycle over, producing more conflict. This is called the *feedback principle.*

The Process of Conflict Ministry

Conflict ministry is the multiple actions of a person seeking to apply the Christian principles of forgiveness, love, and reconciliation to conflict in such a way that Christian growth results for the persons involved. It is a constellation of steps one takes in the face of conflict. Its ultimate objective is reconciliation in Jesus Christ for all of the parties to the conflict.

Each of these steps is related to our process of conflict described above. In Figure 1-3 each of the steps of conflict ministry has been visualized. Start with the first step on the left of the diagram and follow the process with us.

Step 1: Spotting Potential for Conflict

Conflict ministry begins with an awareness of developing conflict. It is quite difficult for some persons to be sensitive to the conditions which foreshadow approaching storms in human relations.

The sources of an ability to "read" the signs of potential conflict are experience, rationality, and intuition. One who has lived through a fight can decipher the conditions of approaching difficulty. Through reason one can sometimes see that some actions or decisions are inadequate to resolve the issues dividing a group; hence, struggle will emerge to satisfy all in the group. A few persons are capable of intuitive feeling about emerging contests within

Figure 1-3: The Conflict Ministry Process

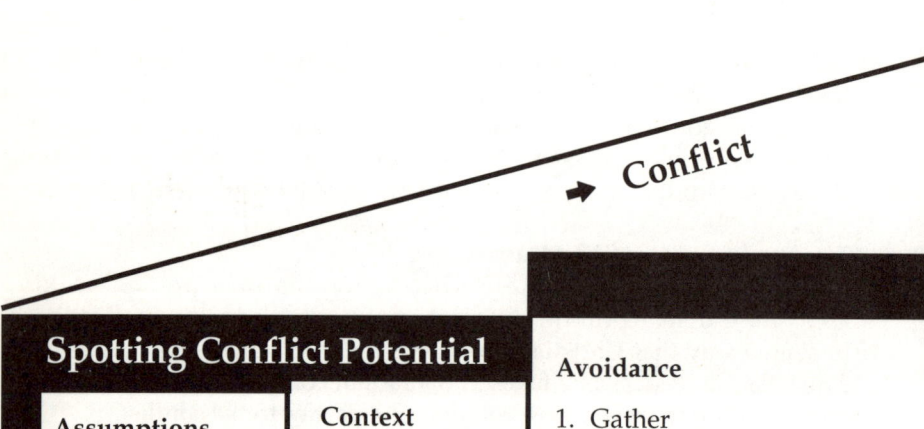

PANORAMA: THE CONFLICT MINISTRY PROCESS

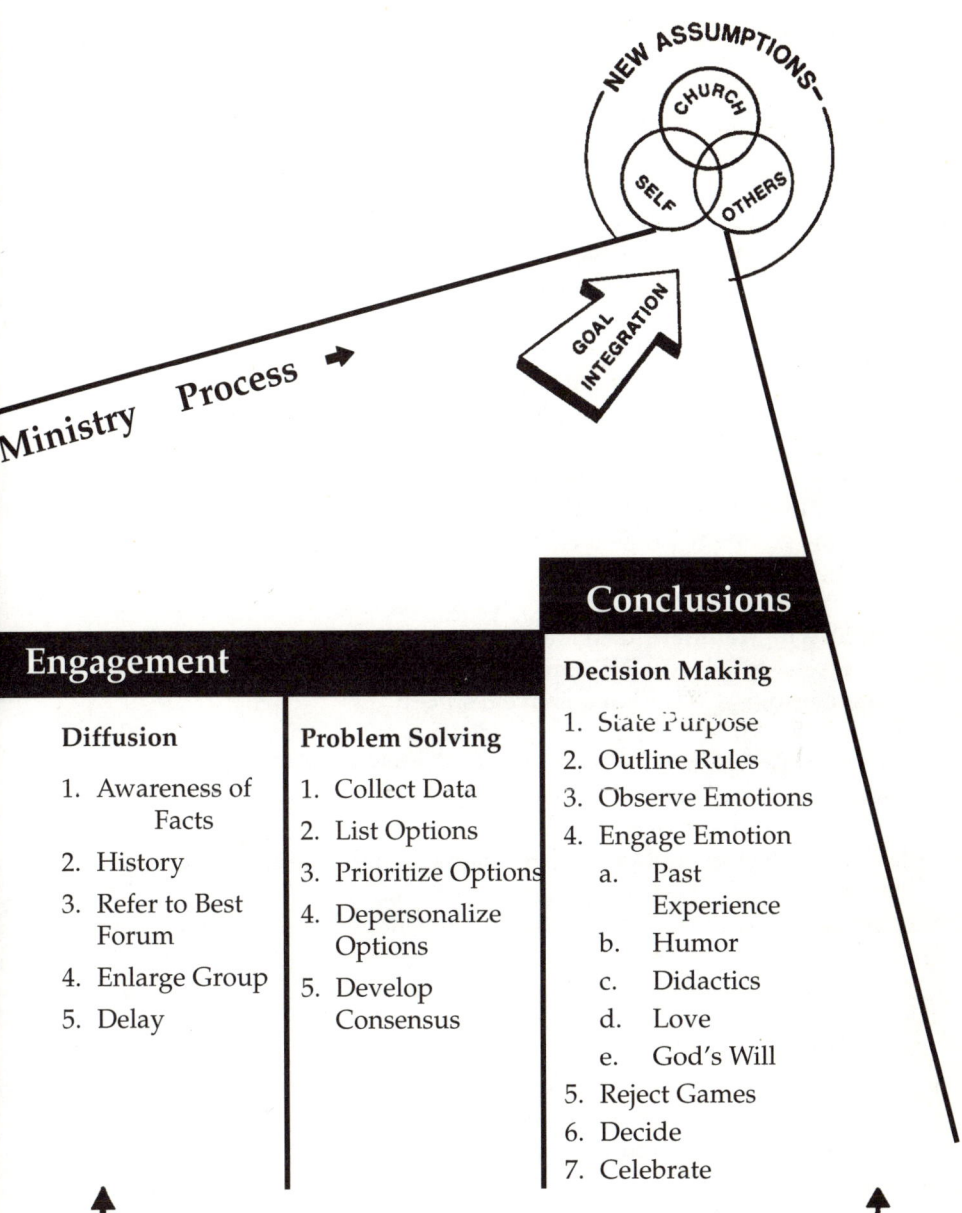

a church. While we cannot give you either the on-the-job training or intuition useful for spotting potential conflict, we can offer suggestions regarding a rational understanding of what is happening.

First, conflict potential can be spotted in the assumptions persons make about conflict. Assumptions are educated guesses about the way things work. They mold what persons do when facing difficult times. One develops these guesses about conflict from thoughts and feelings about conflict. Assumptions influence how we act when faced with conflict.

Assumptions about conflict may cause one to view its consequences as positive or negative. The more negative one's assumptions about conflict are, the more difficult it will be to face conflict productively.

The assumptions of this book can be stated rather simply. They are:
1. The quality of human relationship within a group affects the degree of conflict within it. The more people are aware of each other's assumptions, the more nearly they can work together. Many conflicts in churches could be avoided if more time were spent building relationships before working on tasks. Lyman Coleman says a group ought to use at least one fourth of its time getting to know one another.
2. Churches, like families and associates in work and play, experience conflict. Conflict is a facet of every human group.
3. Conflict within churches can have either positive or negative results for the persons involved. The commitment of individuals in conflict to positive results will lead to positive results.
4. Clergy and laity can learn how to understand and to diagnose the conflict within a church. The more adequately a church is prepared to deal with conflict, the more likely conflict is to be a positive experience. You cannot do much of the work of conflict ministry after conflict has occurred. You do not give history and provide training when people are experiencing the stress of differences. One experienced conflict minister said, "When I am tense I want to talk about the problem, not what should have been done."
5. Effective verbal and nonverbal communication within intimate relationships is the most appropriate means for dealing with conflict within the church.
6. Wise decisions concerning conflict can lead to Christian growth toward maturity for the persons involved.

Do not make the judgment that these assumptions encourage conflict-producing behavior. Neither do they make conflict pleasant. Some of the actions required of meaningful conflict ministry are difficult and painful at the time. Their results, however, are less painful than the consequences of inaction.

Open communication about past experience, feelings, and behavior is

essential if assumptions are to be understood. A major task of the conflict minister is the encouraging of a dialogue concerning conflict with fellow Christians. The following are appropriate questions for the conflict minister to raise before or during situations of conflict affecting individuals or groups.
1. To what degree can these persons communicate their past experiences of conflict with others?
2. What folklore or common expressions emerge whenever conflict appears within this group? Colloquial expressions such as "Better let sleeping dogs lie"; "Don't stir up a hornet's nest"; "He bit off more than he can chew"; and "let's not reinvent the wheel" reveal assumptions persons believe.
3. Who are the authority figures who are mentioned as the guides for handling such situations? If they are not leaders of the church at the time of conflict, trouble lies ahead. A statement like, "Pastor Johnson always said we should pray about these kinds of issues before discussing them" may indicate distrust of the present pastor. Parents, teachers, ministers, and key leaders who are accepted as models reveal the values and attitudes persons have. If you have some understanding of how those personalities function, intuitive judgments can be made about responses to a specific concern.
4. Is there a capacity within the group for making changes in their assumptions? Factors such as age, educational level, attitudinal flexibility, and acceptance of differing options condition the ability to change.
5. What is the feeling tone which emerges within individuals and groups in the face of conflict? Whenever things do not go smoothly does anger erupt? Do some withdraw from the discussion? Is there silence?

Examine the assumptions brought to conflict situations. They are one indication of the potential for conflict in a group.

A second aspect of understanding conflict potential involves studying the context for conflict. Within a congregation there is a balance of personal and organizational relationships which may contribute either to the stimulation and continuation of conflict or to its conclusion. Let us explore the nature of these interactions. The components of the conflict environment are:
- *Prior events* of conflict;
- Quality of *personal interaction* within the church;
- Organization of the *structural life* of the church; and
- Degree of *stress* within and between church members or stress put upon structures by the larger community.

How can an understanding of each of these aid us in observing potential conflict? *Prior experience* with conflict in all areas of our lives teaches us how to handle conflict in the church. If both our assumptions and previous experience

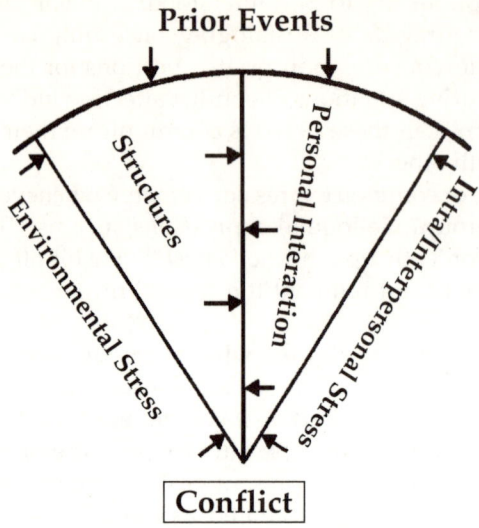

Figure 1-4: Context for Conflict

with conflict are negative, we will avoid it in the church.

Family experiences condition behavior. Perhaps you grew up in a family which denied conflict feelings. Often when you became angry or fought with a friend your parents reminded you, often angrily, "Don't do that! Nice children do not fight." Remembering these childhood feelings now causes you to feel as an adult that you should not be angry with anyone. If you encounter persons in the church whose prior experience encouraged open expression of feelings, you will likely feel threatened by them.

We believe many in the church have been hurt by previous experiences with conflict. They fear it. They avoid it. Certain words we have used in conferences echo a negative response:

fight *confrontation*
controversy *upset*
anger *conflict*

Some congregational histories are conflict-laden. Few major decisions have been made in the past without hurt to someone. The more painful the prior experience of either persons or congregations has been, the more cautiously must conflict be handled by any church group.

Conflict can occur only in the context of *personal interactions.* Usually, conflict is a function of trust and openness. Both are required for the risks posed by dissension to be taken. Strangers seldom fight. Conflict is most likely within families, business partnerships, groups with a lengthy history of personal care for individuals within it, and organizations which have fostered deep personal relationships. It is for this reason that churches are especially susceptible to conflict. The atmosphere of intimacy in religious groups often creates an expectation that relationships can be taken for granted. Internal or external change may provide challenges that an intimate group assumes will never rend its life.

George Williams and Joe Miller had been good friends as they grew up together. Both were successful businessmen in their community and leaders in their church. Joe was chairman of the building committee, leading in construction of totally new facilities. George was a deacon. When the plans were presented for approval to the church in business session, George suggested a change in the arrangement of the kitchen. After considerable discussion, the church approved the original plan, which infuriated George. He stamped from the meeting in anger.

The pastor of six months visited George the next day and criticized his behavior. What the pastor did not know, however, was that George and Joe had become alienated outside the church. George's daughter was married to Joe's brother. Only a few months before, the brothers had contested each other in court over a business contract. George felt his son-in-law had been treated unfairly and could not accept what he thought of as another victory for Joe. He never attended the church again after that business session. In this conflict stresses of personal interaction outside the church had become part of the church's agenda.

Conflict occurs most often in congregations in which there is a deep commitment to the church. The more deeply ingrained is the sense of ownership about what is happening, the more possible is conflict. Apathy is a sure guarantee of a conflict-free setting. Persons who do not care about their faith are unlikely to exhibit enough energy to act upon it. Corpses do not fight!

Structures are a part of the context of conflict. How a church is organized will either facilitate healthy or unhealthy conflict. Some structures produce conflict because they are based upon competition between groups as their method of organization. Others are designed to eliminate the communication necessary for health.

Structures become conflict-producing when there is disagreement about or misunderstanding of the goals and directions of a congregation's life. A consensus about what Anderson and Jones call "core mission or primary task"[10] is needed for maximum ministry effectiveness. Many congregations never settle this most important of community life issues. They divide into factions emphasizing evangelism, missions, quality education, or personal growth as their core mission. To do such is to rob the church of energy for achieving any substantive tasks.

Conflict will be found in those churches which fail to give attention to the survival needs of the church organization. Ordained clergy and laity alike decry the enormous investment of time needed for administration in a church. Yet to leave this dimension of ministry undone is to invite disaster. The time required to develop workable descriptions of committee tasks, budget appropriate resources to each task, and determine accountability for their completion is far less than is needed for restoring the broken relationships created by unhealthy conflict. Every church will have a meeting place, some organization, a budget, and policies for guiding its life.

A final dimension of how structures affect conflict concerns decision making. If conflict ministry is taken seriously, one will look for conflict potential in the way decisions are made. The less consensus in a decision, the more the potential for conflict. An expanded discussion of organizational conflict may be found in chapter 4.

The final variable in the context of conflict is *stress*. Stress is the pressure of change. It may be environmental stress which the church experiences because of community change. It may be the internal stress of job or family pressures with which one cannot cope. It may be the stress of changes in interpersonal relationships.

Stress, whether external or internal, is the factor which brings a conflict event into focus. Whenever the structures or personal relations of a congregation are overstressed, conflict is potentially present. More focus is given to this aspect of conflict in chapter 2.

These are the two variables one must look for in spotting conflict potential: the assumptions people bring to conflict and the context within which it occurs. Too complicated, you say? Not really. As you become observant, by listening and by relying on your intuition about what is happening it will become increasingly apparent when conflict is developing. Now for step 2.

Step 2: Avoid Conflict, with Integrity

When the potential for conflict is high, one has two choices. One can either ignore the situation, so that the momentum of the moment results in conflict; or one can act in such a way that either conflict is avoided or handled constructively.

The first of these choices is a *reactive* style of ministry. It assumes the minister is simply to respond to whatever happens.

The second choice is a *proactive* style of ministry. When the minister observes developing conflict, he or she acts with integrity in such a way as to influence the results of any encounter between persons.

Avoidance is a proactive form of conflict ministry if it is attempted before conflict has crystallized into a public event of encounter. Avoidance is a healthy style of ministry during the stage when conflict potential is present. If the conflict emerges into a publicly observable event, it is too late for an avoidance strategy.

Many avoidance strategies do not work. Some of these unsuccessful strategies are the denial of the existence of conflict, attempts to suppress conflict, and withdrawal from conflict into silence or nonparticipation. Each is a nonproductive avoidance act which will probably ensure more serious conflict.

Productive avoidance strategies, however, help a group find appropriate ways to surface their conflict into the public arena for reconciliation. How can one avoid conflict, with integrity?

1. Ask for more information about the potential conflict. Many conflicts emerge because of misinformation or lack of information regarding an issue. Be sure that all known facts are available to a group before conflict is surfaced for public discussion.
2. Ensure enough time for the conflict to be managed. Many conflicts can be resolved if there is sufficient time for all parties to work together on their differences. Delay is one avoidance strategy which gives persons the time they need to function wisely.
3. Assess the level of maturity of the individuals or group facing conflict. Management specialists Paul Hersey and Kenneth Blanchard suggest different leadership styles are required for differing levels of maturity. They say maturity consists of two factors. The first is the willingness to accept responsibility for setting and achieving goals. Mature persons are highly motivated, willing to be held accountable for decisions, tasks, and failures. The second factor is the ability to accept responsibility. Some actions require a certain amount of training, experience, or natural skill to be accomplished. The third factor of maturity is self-confidence. The most mature individuals are those who are willing to accept responsibility, able to accept responsibility, and who feel confident they can fulfill that responsibility with self-respect. Those least mature are neither willing, able, nor self-confident in accepting responsibility for themselves.[11]

    There is an added spiritual dimension to maturity in the church. Those who are mature express their abilities as gifts of the Holy Spirit (1 Cor. 12:4-11; Eph. 4:11-14). Their willingness to serve and their sense of self-esteem are of the Spirit (Rom. 8:9-11; Gal. 2:20). Mature Christians behave wisely and responsibly in honor of the Christ who dwells within.

    Finally, there are psychological dimensions to immaturity. Some individuals choose to act as perpetual "troublemakers" for whom specialized ministry is required. Some people choose to live disordered lives, refusing the forgiving grace of God for their sins. Clinical psychologist Paul Schmidt has identified a number of "character disorders" which lead to paranoid, obsessive, hysterical, aggressive, apathetic, temperamental, compulsive, impulsive dependent, or manipulative styles of behavior.[12] Group life can be developed to isolate such persons so their problems can be dealt with in an individual setting.

4. Avoidance will allow the conflict minister to gauge the emotional temperature of the conflict. Emotional level is the least controllable factor in conflict. If emotional intensity builds beyond the level of information available or the time available, the conflict can be avoided by focusing the emotion away from the conflict. For example, a group moving toward conflict may develop high levels of anger. If the leader of the group observes this, a simulation game of another conflict may be attempted as a release of the tension. Humor, competitive group activities, or change of agenda can be used to allow the dissipation of anger that is hurting others.

The purpose of avoidance is not to run from conflict. Rather, it is to anticipate the most appropriate way to resolve conflict at a time when the issues can be resolved with maximum benefit for all parties involved. Avoidance with integrity is a proactive strategy applied to potential conflict before it has developed into a conflict event.

Step 3: Engage Conflict Events Productively

Avoidance is a strategy for engaging potential conflict before it is fully developed. Once conflict has surfaced publicly, the conflict minister must employ a different set of strategies for engaging it. Figure 1-3 shows that this step is to be taken after "the event" is in process.

A conflict event is an encounter between persons and/or groups in which their differences are either observed by others or discussed by those in conflict with others. It is conflict potential crystallized and visible in public. A conflict event is a symbol of many different feelings, ideas, and opinions which can be described and dated. Many examples of conflict events can be mentioned: an argument between a husband and wife; an issue which separates a congregation into factions; a vote by a church to dismiss the pastor; picketing of a business establishment which practices racial discrimination; a church body divided on whether to ordain women clergy.

How does the conflict minister respond when conflict is clearly visible? The choices are between strategies designed to help those in conflict move toward constructive growth through goal integration on a higher plan or toward destructive disintegration of persons and relationships. Some strategies help persons grow into more healthy Christian disciples. Others do not.

Unhealthy strategies of engagement include fright, flight, or fight. Healthy strategies involve some form of problem solving which brings freedom.

When conflict immobilizes a group, *fright* is the response. Some persons are so fearful of conflict they refuse to acknowledge its presence in their midst. Denial is a fright strategy of nonengagement of conflict. Passive pastoral leaders often expend enormous amounts of energy attempting to ensure a placid church life by denying all problems. Reactive deferment of conflict is a fright strategy, for it assumes that if one keeps putting off conflict it will go away. It seldom does.

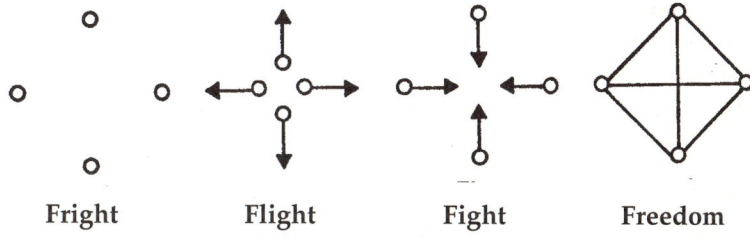

Fright **Flight** **Fight** **Freedom**

Figure 1-5: Forms of Engagement

Flight is a second approach to conflict events. One can simply withdraw from the arena of conflict. Withdrawal happens when people change church memberships in order to keep from becoming involved. Withholding of money for church programs, refusing to vote on either side of an issue, and nonparticipation in church activities are withdrawal actions. Many inactive church members have become so because of conflicts they have fled.

Fighting is the most harmful form of response to conflict. Fighting includes a variety of actions. Repression is a fight strategy as one group in the majority constantly overrules a powerless minority in their efforts to be heard. Subversion is the effort to undermine the majority of leadership by underground campaigns exaggerating issues or engaging in character assassination. Fight strategies can degenerate into violence. They do not develop Christian character or Christlike behavior within the church community.

There are productive forms of engagement which should be employed when conflict events occur. Their goal is the development of group *freedom* to conclude their conflicts on a higher plane of Christian love. The first of these is *diffusion*. Diffusion is a strategy employed by conflict ministers when the conflict event

has come to the group as a surprise or is concentrated within a small part of the congregation. It is at work when the following steps are taken.
1. Test the total group's awareness of the facts which are at issue in the conflict event. Until all the members of the group in conflict are informed of the nature of the conflict, the issues at hand, and the information needed to understand the issues, healthy decisions making cannot occur.
2. Ask someone to explain the history of the conflict. If the group understands how the current situation came into being, an awareness of the complexity of the issues being discussed can counter the apparent simplicity of the conflict.
3. Refer the conflict to the appropriate forum for discussion, recommendation, or resolution. Some conflicts emerge in large groups before they have been discussed in a smaller forum, such as a standing committee or task group. Some individuals interpose personal agendas that need resolution in a face-to-face counseling setting. Often the best diffusion strategy is to refuse discussion of the conflict issue until it has been referred to a more appropriate forum for discussion than the one in which it originated.
4. Enlarge the conflict groups with responsible others. On occasion the dynamics of a given group make it impossible for healthy conclusions of concerns to occur. A committee that is becoming dysfunctional can regain its health through the addition of other responsible leaders who can bring new insights to the group. A conflict between two deacons is often resolved by drawing a responsible third party into the conflict. A group may need the outside help of a referee or third party specialist. Enlarge the group in conflict.
5. Delay action on the conflict until a healthy process of conflict ministry has been attempted. Timing is often the most crucial factor in conflict. Conflict can be diffused by delaying discussion, decision, or attempted resolution until a longer time has been spent in analyzing the conflict.

Once unexpected conflict has been diffused, the process of conclusion can begin. We call this process *problem-solving analysis.* The purpose of analysis is to explore the problem before a group in such a way as to allow the group to make the best possible decision concerning that problem.

Problem-solving analysis moves through five steps.
1. Collect all of the necessary information regarding the problem which is at the root of the conflict. This includes facts, feelings, and opinions.
2. Conceptualize all of the potential options which may be chosen as solutions to the problem. An option includes the action or decision which must be made, the potential results of that action or decision, and the risks for failure in it.

3. List each of the options in the order of their apparent priority. Which resolves the problems best with the fewest negative consequences? This we call the *principle of tradeoffs*.
4. Depersonalize the options. The selection of a given option must be separated from feelings of personal acceptance or rejection by individuals in the conflict.
5. Develop a consensus of group support for the option or options which most nearly resolve the conflict. Compromise is often required among the parties for a consensus to emerge.

When the process of problem-solving analysis has been completed by the appropriate forum, a group is ready to resolve its conflict. This is done as a decision or action taken by the group as a healthy response to the conflict within it. Decision making is the symbolic act which clarifies to parties in conflict that they have achieved a workable solution as Christian partners.

Step 4: Conclude Conflict Through Responsible Decision Making

The conflict minister is most visible in the conflict ministry process at the point of those decisions which are made in response to dissension. The effective conflict minister must exercise authoritative control and sensitive leadership as a guide to the group as it works toward a healthy decision. Briefly, the responsibilities of the conflict minister at this step of the process are as follows:

1. State clearly the purposes of the meeting and the nature of the decisions to be made.
2. Outline the ground rules which are to be followed in the course of decision making.
3. Be sensitive to the emotional reactions of the group to the decision-making process. These are communicated verbally and nonverbally through anger, withdrawal, denial, fighting, and submission.
4. Engage the emotion exhibited at several levels. This can be done through the sharing of a past experience where conflict has been resolved, a personal testimony of change in behavior resulting from good decisions, the communication of loving concern for members of the group, use of teaching about appropriate expressions of feeling, and appeal to the higher purposes of God's will for the actions of the group.
5. Refuse to play engagement games to influence the decision. An engagement game is an appeal for emotional support for one's personal position rather than a search for the best possible decision for all involved. Some of the games leaders play are:
    "Suffering Servant"—I am doing this for your best good at great personal sacrifice.

"Isn't It Wonderful"—If you do this it will be the most wonderful thing that has ever happened to me.

"Paternal Grandfather"—Now I am sure you will want to do this because I know how much it will bless your life in the years to come.

"Since I Came"—Our church has been such a wonderful fellowship since I came, and I know you will not do anything to destroy what I have done.

"If You Really Loved Me"—This is the best game of all for it puts guilt upon all who will not support your decision. It makes of them unloving persons.

6. Give the group freedom to decide. Conflict ministers must trust those with whom they work to make good decisions when the above processes have been at work.

Much more could be said about healthy decision making. Ministry continues after a decision as well. These dimensions are given much fuller explanation in chapter 4.

Step 5: Celebrate the Conclusion of Conflict

We have deliberately chosen not to talk about "conflict resolution" or "conflict solutions" in this book. Each of these denotes the idea of decisions which perfectly satisfy everyone. We have seen few conflicts resolved or solved. Given the concept of trade-off we mentioned in step 3, we believe there are negative consequences of most decisions for someone. When those negatively affected are willing to support a decision because it is recognized by all parties in conflict as the best possible outcome available to the group, we can say the conflict has been concluded. The conflict ceases. Some forms of engagement result in lingering conflict or dissension. One cannot say a conclusion has been reached. There are three kinds of conclusions.

Win-Win conclusions are decisions which all parties in the conflict support as the best possible decision of the group. It represents consensus in the group and is the healthiest form of conclusion.

Win-Lose conclusions occur where there is majority rule but no consensus regarding the outcome of decision making.

Lose-Lose conclusions put the conflict to rest, but only because all parties are willing to give up chosen alternatives for ending the conflict. It usually occurs when conflict has emerged in an inappropriate forum or poor processes of decision making have been followed. This is the least healthy form of conclusion, for one group wins by breaking the rules of fairness.

When a conflict has been concluded in a win-win way, the entire group can move forward toward its mission as a Christian community. Its goals have

PANORAMA: THE CONFLICT MINISTRY PROCESS 33

been incorporated into its life more deeply. It will function with greater resolve to be the church in its setting. Such is a cause for Christian celebration.

Closure of the conflict experience should be accomplished in the context of prayer and praise. Many acts of Christian celebration can be employed to symbolize the resolve of the person in conflict to move forward toward the "prize of the upward call of God in Christ Jesus" (Phil. 3:14). Singing, circles of friendship, celebrations of the Lord's Supper, prayer, or small-group sharing might be appropriate methods for celebrating the victory of concluded conflict.

Here is the framework we have developed for doing conflict ministry. We have tried to make this process as simple as possible. Conflict, however, is a complex reality. For this reason these steps must be followed with flexibility. The remaining chapters expand aspects of the overall model. We begin with an effort to understand the role of internal stress upon conflict in the church.

Glossary

Assumptions: educated guesses about life and the way things work. They influence how persons will behave in a particular setting. One's assumptions about conflict influence whether it is viewed positively or negatively.

Avoidance: a strategy for influencing the quality of conflict ministry before conflict occurs. Nonproductive avoidance strategies include the denial of conflict, attempts to suppress conflict, and withdrawal from conflict. Productive avoidance strategies include information gathering, delay, and stress management for individuals in conflict.

Conflict: a situation in which two or more persons desire and pursue goals which they perceive as being attainable by one or the other, but not by both.

Conflict Conclusions: the results of engagement with conflict. Conclusions may be win-win outcomes in which all parties gain from the conflict, win-lose outcomes in which only one party gains, and lose-lose in which neither party in conflict gains from the experience.

Conflict Event: a public encounter between persons in conflict which symbolizes the existence and the character of their differences.

Conflict Ministry: the actions of a person or group seeking to apply the Christian principles of forgiveness, love and reconciliation to conflict in such a way that Christian growth results for the persons involved.

Conflict Situation: a setting in which the potential for conflict is high. Particular actions or decisions will result in conflict between persons, groups, or organizations.

Diffusion: a strategy of spreading unexpected conflict through a group by referral to a committee, gathering additional information, enlarging the group dealing with it, or delaying response until healthy processes can be employed.

Engagement: the actions one takes to bring conflict to a conclusion by the application of a conflict ministry strategy to the conflict event. Avoidance, diffusion, and problem-solving analysis are effective strategies of engagement.

Engagement Game: an appeal for emotional support of one's personal position rather than a search for consensus.

Problem-Solving Analysis: a process of seeking a consensus conclusion to conflict by gathering needed information about the conflict, developing alternative conclusions, examining the trade-offs of each conclusion and selecting the best conclusions for the benefit of the total group.

Strategy: an overall process one applies to attempt to bring conflict to a conclusion.

Stress: the effects of external forces which upset the physical, emotional, or spiritual balance within persons, resulting in a struggle to adapt to those forces. It is conflict which persons feel within themselves.

Notes:

[1] See Werner Foerster, "eirene," *Theological Dictionary of the New Testament*, ed. Gerhard Kittel, trans. and ed. by Geoffrey W. Bromiley (Grand Rapids: Wm. B. Eerdmans Publishing Co., 1965), II, 400-417; Douglas James Harris, *Shalom: The Biblical Concept of Peace* (Grand Rapids: Baker Book House, 1971) and Jack L. Stotts, *Shalom: The Search for a Peaceable City* (Nashville: Abingdon Press, 1973), pp. 97-114. In the Old Testament *shalom* referred primarily to the well-being which came from God and applied more specifically to the concerns of groups, such as the nation, than to an individual spiritual inwardness. In the New Testament *eirene* carried with it the same idea of well-being in opposition to disorder (1 Cor. 14:33). It also referred to the final salvation of the whole person (in a sense equivalent to eternal life), the opposite of enmity (*exthra*) with God, harmonious relationships between persons (Eph. 4:3, Jas. 3:18), and as peace of soul.

[2] Sherman E. Johnson, "Matthew," *The Interpreter's Bible*, ed. George Arthur Buttrick (New York: Abingdon Press, 1951), VII, 479.

[3] The concept of *henosis* or unity underlies the divine pattern of relationship for the sexes in Genesis 2:23-24 according to Derrick Sherwin Bailey, *The Mystery of Love and Marriage* (New York: Harper & Brothers Publishers, 1952) in this excellent study of the meaning of "one flesh."

[4] William Butler Yeats, "The Second Coming," *Selected Poems and Two Plays of William Butler Yeats*, ed. M. L. Rosenthal (New York: Collier Books, 1962), p. 91.

[5] John A. T. Robinson, *The Human Face of God* (Philadelphia: Lawrence Hill, 1973) is a thorough study of the meaning of incarnation and the human struggles encountered by Jesus, without denying His uniqueness. Conservative Christians will disagree with the nature of his approach to the relationship between humanity and uniqueness.

[6] Jürgen Moltmann, *The Crucified God: The Cross Of Christ as the Foundation of Criticism of Christian Theology* (New York: Harper and Row, 1974) has demonstrated the social aspects of the meaning of the cross within the framework of a profound theology. T. B. Maston, *Why Live the Christian Life?* (Nashville: Thomas Nelson, Inc., 1974), pp. 157-187, sees the cross as a symbol of Christian living. Such a life is one of self-denial and self-sacrifice. It is a commitment to inevitable tension between the way of God and the way of the world.

PANORAMA: THE CONFLICT MINISTRY PROCESS 35

[7] Since the publication of Jürgen Moltmann, *The Theology of Hope* (London: SCM Press, 1967) the theme of eschatological hope has been one of the most crucial in contemporary theology. The importance of this doctrine is developed by him in the framework of a liberation ethic which relates the end to critical social issues and thus avoids the other worldliness of much eschatological thought.

[8] Speed B. Leas and Paul L. Kittlaus, *Church Fights: Managing Conflict in the Local Church* (Philadelphia: The Westminster Press, 1973), p. 28.

[9] *The Dimensions of Human Conflict*, comp. by Ross Stagner (Detroit: Wayne State University Press, 1967), p. 136, quoted in *Church Fights: Managing Conflicts in the Local Church*, pp. 28-29.

[10] James D. Anderson and Ezra E. Jones, *The Management of Ministry* (New York: Harper and Row, 1978), p. 182.

[11] Paul Hersey and Kenneth H. Blanchard, *Management of Organizational Behavior: Utilizing Human Resources*, 3rd ed. (Englewood Cliffs: Prentice-Hall, Inc. 1977), pp. 161-163.

[12] Paul F. Schmidt, *Coping With Difficult People*, Christian Care Books, ed. Wayne E. Oates (Philadelphia: The Westminster Press, 1980).

The Continuing

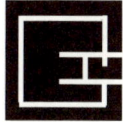

Education Unit •

Assignment

1. The authors describe conflict ministry as a "process." Explain what they mean and describe the relationship between conflict and communication.

2. In what way is our understanding of conflict in the world and the church informed by the doctrine of creation. How would you justify the author's assertion that conflict is "necessary."

3. Identify and describe the four sources of conflict in the church.

4. What are the two variables you can look for which will help in spotting conflict potential. Explain.

5. Explain why conflict is more likely to occur in congregations in which there is a deep commitment to the church.

6. Cite situations which would justify "avoidance" as a strategy for engaging conflict compared to a "diffusion" strategy. Describe the process by which you would bring the latter to "conclusion."

Chapter 2

Stress: The Root of Conflict

Stress is a life experience. The pressures of competition at school, work, and social circles create external demands upon us that shape the decisions we must make. The accelerating pace of life, the complexity of change which surrounds us, and the feelings of helplessness which confront many create the conditions for a kind of internal *angst* or anxiety which manifests itself in numerous ways in our lives.

What Is Stress?

Stress is a complicated concept. If you look at the variety of people you know, it is interesting to note the differences of reaction they make to similar events in their lives. The death of a husband occurs in two different families. The reactions of the widows will be unique to each. Such an event is overpowering in both instances and the pain of grief is evident for both. Yet, six months later the two widows are making entirely different adjustments. The pain has been no less intense for either. But for one widow the event has been accepted as one which cannot be changed. She is striving to develop new patterns of relationships, to set new goals for her life, and make decisions that will allow her to continue living with purpose, even if she must do so alone. The other widow responds quite the opposite. The death of her husband is unacceptable to her. She turns inward and becomes isolated from others. She carries her grief alone and insists upon living as though her husband were still alive. Soon she finds herself hospitalized with serious physical problems, requiring major surgery. Her hope is that she may die and join her husband.

Both individuals experienced the same stressor—death. Why they responded differently may be the result of many factors, such as their personalities, attitudes toward death, degree of preparedness for the death of their mates, their financial security as widows, the family support experienced during grief, and the nature of their church's ministry to them.

Perhaps their illustration can provide a basis for examining how stress functions in our lives. Most of the research on stress has examined its physiological bases and manifestations. Hans Selye, a Canadian research physician, has been one of the pioneers in discovering the physical mechanisms at work when stress occurs.[1] Others have focused upon the psychological, environmental, and social aspects of stress.[2] It may even be related to the timed cycles of physical processes that occur in the body daily.[3] Stress is also related to the spiritual realm of life. The harm of stress to persons is a direct result of human sin. Chapter 1 emphasized the origin of all harm to human relationships in the fall—the rebellion of all men and women against God's intention as Creator. While there is no unanimous agreement within these multiple approaches as to the nature of stress, general concurrence can be found on the following emphases.

First, any event in life can act as a *stressor*. Stress is essential for life. The motivation to achieve as well as the pressure one feels in achieving are its by-products. The physical stimulus to respond to danger as well as the depression of an overtaxed body are results of stress. The stress mechanism helps the body fight disease and contributes to certain illnesses. Nancy Gross suggests: "A stressless life would be a vegetable life, so monotonous, so tedious, so uneventful, so unrelievedly placid, that it would undoubtedly lead to the living death of utter and complete boredom."[4] Life without stress is impossible. Disaster, captivity, surgery, heat, noise, work, childhood traumas, movies, fatigue, and a host of other daily realities bring stress to the human organism.

Second, individuals will respond differently to the same stressors. A change in employment will be experienced by two families quite differently. For one it may be seen as a new challenge offering more excitement, additional income, and new relationships. Another person may experience such a change as added responsibility, uprootedness from established friends, and the possibility of failure. Within a family this change may be perceived differently. A husband sees a transfer to the corporate headquarters as opportunity, while for the children and wife it is viewed as another series of adjustments to a new house, new schools, new church, new shops, and a new community.[5] A given individual's ability to handle stressors may vary depending upon numerous factors such as timing, place, previous experience, spiritual well-being, and the environmental pressures upon him or her at a given moment. As Gross emphasized: "Stress itself is an objective, measurable fact, but our reactions to it are highly subjective.... The stress that makes one man ill can be exhilarating to another, and even those whose tolerance for stress is high will vary in their reactions to it depending on its specific cause."[6]

Personality factors and cultural expectations are significant factors influencing how individuals respond to situations of stress. Harvard University researchers studied four basic types of psychological reactions to stress. Each group of persons with similar responses shared similar personality characteristics.

The first group showed little emotion or reaction to the stresses they faced. They were *strongly authoritarian* persons who tended to handle new situations rigidly and with little doubt; these were most effective in completing tasks under stress. A second group externalized anger toward others or toward objects when under stress. This group tended to be slightly more flexible in concepts and approaches than the first and functioned rather well in handling stress. Group 3 was able to function at a more moderate level when stressed. This group tended to become angry also. But its anger was *directed inwardly*. These persons were relatively nonauthoritarian in relationships, sensitive toward others, and flexible in adjusting to changes. A fourth group was found to be very *anxious* and *frustrated* by stress. Marked physical changes occurred, for when subjected to stress and emotional states became so elevated that group members were unable to perform tasks while stressed. This group tended to be very sensitive toward others, unable to relate authoritatively, and manifested considerable lack of self-assurance.[7]

These same responses can be noted among those who are involved in the church. A few people seem to be able to handle most events with relative ease. They show little emotion in the face of controversy or change. Another group becomes outwardly angry, directing their anger toward the pastor, church leaders, or the congregation as a whole. Others become equally angry but blame themselves for the stress they feel. Their anger is internalized, never discussed, and often displaced at a later time when the issues are different and unrelated. Withdrawal may be the reaction of the fourth group. Their dysfunction in the face of conflict leads to the desire to leave the source of conflict. The same person who may be able to offer sensitive care toward others reacts with hurt to the existence of stress within the personal or organizational relationships of the church. Varied reactions to stress should be anticipated by church leaders whenever new ideas are presented.

Third, there is a relationship between changes in life situations and stress. Individuals have varying capacities to assimilate change: each has a "threshold of change" beyond which one cannot live without damage from stress. Selye states, "It seems to be one of the most fundamental laws regulating the activities of complex living beings that no one part of the body must be disproportionately overworked for a long time."[8] Either the constancy of the same stimuli or the constancy of change in stimuli can be sufficiently powerful to alter the best performance or decision-making capacities of individuals.

Thomas H. Holmes and Richard H. Rahe have studied this relationship for several years and concluded that there is a direct relationship between the changes one experiences and the likelihood of illness. By studying the life-situation patterns of many different groups they have constructed a Social Readjustment Rating Scale whereby one can estimate the likelihood of serious illness based upon changes in life situations. By examining Table 2-1 you can calculate your own stress situation.[9] Each of the life events has been given a numerical value. If one totals the numerical values of all of the changes experienced in a given year, some general estimate of susceptibility to illness can be made. The higher one's total score, the greater the possibility of illness in the future. Blue Cross-Blue Shield estimates a stress sum of more than 300 points accumulated within one year will result in a 90 percent chance of health change within two years, 150-300 points in a 50 percent chance of health change, and below 150 is a 30 percent chance.

Congregations and ministers who are committed to a caring ministry to persons will be sensitive in applying this insight. During periods of upheaval, rapid change, or alteration within the lives of people, the need for attention, care, and support will be more intense. Likewise, changes in the sociology of a community, the move of several families to other communities, rapid growth or shifts in leadership may trigger stresses within a congregation. By engaging in a regular check-up of the rate of change, preventive care can be administered to congregations and persons as a prescription for maintaining health and vitality.

Fourth, stress affects the totality of a person. It is impossible to predict the effect which a given stressor may have on persons. Selye called the way we respond to stress the *general adaptation syndrome*.[10] Lazarus called the same pattern *coping*.[11] While the specific reaction we make may be different, there is a general process which occurs. The body is changed as a result of stress. The change alters behavior. In the face of a stressor the mechanism of the body cause hormonal and chemical changes designed to fight the stressors it faces. Such occurs in stages. In the first stage there is an *alarm reaction*. The physiological resources of the body are triggered to fight the stressors which are acting upon it. In the second stage there is *resistance* as the body adapts to its stressors by distributing their effects as broadly as possible throughout its mechanism. In the third stage there is *exhaustion* if the body is not successfully able to cope with the stressors which affect it. When stressors overcome the body's resistive reaction, illnesses such as ulcers, heart attack, high blood pressure, arthritis, and kidney disease occur. Aging and eventually death are the final consequences of stress.

Fifth, persons can learn how to control the effects of stress. The advantage of learning how stress works is that one can become a more victorious Christian. Good physical care, the maintenance of disciplines which promote

Table 2-1
Social Readjustment Rating Scale

Rank	Life Event	Mean Value
1	Death of spouse	100
2	Divorce	73
3	Marital separation	65
4	Jail term	63
5	Death of close family member	63
6	Personal injury or illness	53
7	Marriage	50
8	Fired at work	47
9	Marital reconciliation	45
10	Retirement	45
11	Change in health of family member	44
12	Pregnancy	40
13	Sex difficulties	39
14	Gain of a new family member	39
15	Business readjustment	39
16	Change in financial state	38
17	Death of close friend	37
18	Change to different line of work	36
19	Change in no. of arguments with spouse	35
20	Mortgage over $10,000	31
21	Foreclosure of mortgage or loan	30
22	Change in responsibilities at work	29
23	Son or daughter leaving home	29
24	Trouble with in-laws	29
25	Outstanding personal achievement	28
26	Wife begin or stop work	26
27	Begin or end school	26
28	Change in living conditions	25
29	Revision of personal habits	24
30	Trouble with boss	23
31	Change in work hours or conditions	20
32	Change in residence	20
33	Change in schools	20
34	Change in recreation	19
35	Change in church activities	19
36	Change in social activities	18
37	Mortgage or loan less than $10,000	17
38	Change in sleeping habits	16
39	Change in no. of family get-togethers	15
40	Change in eating habits	15
41	Vacation	13
42	Christmas	12
43	Minor violations of the law	11

emotional health, and practicing Christian prayer and meditation are each stress relieving. In the same way stress affects the totality of a person, the gospel is concerned with the totality of a person. When Jesus grew in wisdom, stature, and favor with God and man (Luke 2:52), He was applying God's will to the whole of His life. Stress becomes a positive source of growth for those who live faith in this whole perspective. Practical suggestions for how churches can be teachers of stress management will be offered in the last section of this chapter.

Thus far in this chapter considerable attention has been given to the concept of stress and several factors related to it. Stress may have positive or negative effects depending upon personality and social factors. Now it is possible to arrive at a definition which encompasses these multiple aspects of what is meant by stress. Stress in the sense it is used in this book refers to the effects of external forces or stimuli (stressors) which upset the physical, emotional, or spiritual balance within persons resulting in a struggle to adapt (cope) to the changes of these forces or stimuli.

Stress is a form of threat which may manifest itself in the following forms:
- *Physical* threat is stress based upon actual or anticipated physical injury, pain, or death.
- *Ego* threat is stress based on actual or anticipated pain to the psychological self.
- *Interpersonal* threat is stress based upon actual or anticipated disruption of social relationships.
- *Environmental* threat is stress based upon a constraining and/or impoverished environment.[12]
- *Spiritual* threat is stress based upon actual or anticipated disruption of those practices which promote a sense of the presence of God in one's life.

How Stress Produces Conflict

What is the relationship between stress and conflict? The idea of stress has been applied to the human organism and its ability to adapt or cope with stressors. By analogy it could be extended also to include relations between persons and within or between groups. However, in this book the focus is upon stress as an individual problem. The effects of how stressed individuals interact with other individuals or groups and how groups themselves function when stressed we are calling "conflict."

Stress is intrapersonal conflict. It forces individuals to choose from among a multitude of options in life how they shall live. These choices are not between a stressed or stressless life. Nancy Gross reminds us of the necessity of stress saying,

> All of us must experience some stress, but to some extent, at least, we can determine for ourselves, by our own choices of a pattern of life, how much and what kind of stress we will endure. Whatever our choice, we must make it in the knowledge that stress is a fundamental fact of life. It is the common denominator of all pressure experience. It is the body's basic pattern of response to all demanding situations. It is a state of being in which all of us live.... And when we use it properly, it gives zest to life.[13]

The key to meaningful life is learning how to live with stress without distress.[14] At times the stress of life becomes more than we can bear. In such situations help is needed. Surely the apostle Paul has such traumas in mind when he admonished the Christians of Galatia to "bear one another's burdens" (Gal. 6:2).

When stress becomes dysfunctional for a person, it has effects upon other persons. The pressures of life spill from the lives of those stressed to others closest to them. The *person experiencing stress within is the root of conflict with others.* Stresses lead to conflict with those held most dear and loved most deeply. Dr. Frederick W. Ilfeld, Jr., assistant clinical professor of psychiatry at the University of California-Davis, has found that the most stressful of life's events are marriage and parenthood—those realities closest to us. [15]

Often the church is the first social grouping to experience the dysfunctions of persons living with unconquered stress. Behaviors of anger, hostility, frustration, hurt, and distance are signals of need that call for response and care. Too often the response is rejection and disassociation because we do not understand the needs of the person who seems always to be instigating "fires of destruction" which someone must extinguish.

Clergy must be sensitive to the stresses they experience also. Overstress among the clergy is a major source of the conflicts churches experience. The role expectations of laity toward ministers are often so naïve they do not allow ministers to experience the same stresses as others. Given the subjective nature of their work and the difficulty of visible measures for their hours of toil, stress becomes one of the acute "occupational hazards" of the profession. The sedentary nature of the tasks of ministry, the long hours of weekly service, the constancy of availability to people, and relatively low financial rewards of the work bear their toll in frustration.[16] No congregation will live up to the expectations of its potential if its ministers live with dysfunctional stress.

Sometimes the stresses are not directly related to ministry so much as the normal pressures of life all of us experience. Consider the experience of an effective and productive pastor who lives with a daily fearfulness of stagnation that robs him of the joy he seeks in ministry. His is the feeling of middle-age depression many experience as a call to seek another vocation, another marriage, or another position of employment.[17] Read his honest confession.

I am 48 years old with 23 years' experience in pastoral ministry. The church I serve is located in a university setting, has an excellent reputation for the quality of its fellowship and the vision of its ministry, and offers numerous opportunities for creative service. I came to this church about four years ago from a larger church in a region where my denomination is relatively strong. I moved because of the challenge of ministry in a section of the country which provided a sense of mission opportunity. Also, two of my three children had married during my former pastorate and had settled in that community to live. They needed the opportunity to develop their own identities which this change in locations offered.

For the past two years I have been deeply troubled by the commonly held feeling that says, "A minister past 45 years of age cannot move except to a less desirable place of service." As a matter of fact, this idea has been dominant in my daily thoughts most of the past two years. I find that I have been conditioned to accept the current philosophy of ministry which considers success to be a steady movement "upward" from smaller to larger churches. I fear I may not be able to move solely because of my age.

The irony of all of this is that there is no need for me to escape a bad situation. The church I serve is excellent in every way in the relationship we share. I have not been disillusioned with conditions in the "pioneer" area nor with the academic community. It seems that I have this need to move simply because I am afraid I cannot move due to my age.

Emotional periods of apathy, melancholia, and fear in intense proportions bother me. Hardly a day passes when I do not think about the possibility that I may not be able to move again. And still there are not inquiries nor committees visiting my church from other places. I know this is an irrational fear. I do not think the adage of immobility after age 45 is true. But I know enough ministers my age who appear to be stuck in their present work that I have not been able to escape this fear. I am trying not to let it immobilize me nor render me ineffective in ministry. I really feel that I am more qualified for ministry now than ever before. I have intensified my efforts to be a good pastor by giving more and more attention to the needs of the congregation. I have sought more quality in preaching, diversity in my devotional practices, involvement in continuing education programs, and have entered into a Doctor of Ministry study program. This is being done to prevent stagnation and to eliminate the possibility that I may become disqualified for any future expanded ministry. Yet the fear remains, constantly surfacing. I know that if this fear is not conquered soon, I will begin to decline as a minister. Yet the fear remains that I am past the point where I can move to another church simply because of my age.

The debilitating effects of stress are evident in this personal account. Few would be able to verbalize these kinds of feelings so openly. What would you suggest is the source of his stress? Is it likely that it is robbing him of effectiveness in ways he may not recognize? What would you suggest to him as the way out of his anxiety?

One of the positive steps congregations and denominational leaders must take if conflict is to be handled productively in the church is providing resources for stress control for clergy. A number of factors need consideration if stress levels are to be lowered among professionals in the church. Included in these are counseling and career assessment resources, study leaves, adequate vacation time, equitable and adequate salaries and support groups. Each minister must be accountable to himself for his stresses by balancing work with pleasure, study with recreation, giving ministry with receiving ministry, and maintaining strong family support. All of these will contribute to a ministry that functions with health and wholeness.[18]

The Church as a Creator of Stress

Conflict ministry begins when churches recognize the stresses of persons and work to provide a supportive atmosphere in which those stresses can be managed. Much of the conflict of group and congregational life within churches could be avoided if over stressed individuals received the care, support, and release they need to control their stresses.

The first ministry churches can perform is to recognize when they are becoming sources of stress to individuals within them. Have you ever known individuals who functioned at an exceedingly high level of control in their occupations and families who were often irritable and dissatisfied whenever they were present in the church? Strained personal relationships between pastors and church members within a fellowship have often occurred as a result of church-related stressors with which the individuals involved had not learned to cope. It may be somewhat unusual to consider this aspect of church life, but an honest examination of how churches add to the pressures of members can help determine positive steps to provide a more adequate ministry to persons. Consider some of the ways in which churches overstress their members.

Unmet expectations and unfulfilled hopes—A congregation which fails to meet the expectations and hopes of its members may discover the loss of participation by those who live with the stress of disappointment. Joseph E. McGrath reviewed more than 200 stress research projects to summarize the themes to be found in their emphases. He says stress is in the eye of the beholder.[19] We are most likely to feel disappointment when we fail attempting those tasks we expect to be stressful, but worth the cost. When we undertake certain actions or goals of a church, a failure to achieve those actions results in stress.

The following case is the description of the relationship between a pastor and family who have discovered that their child has a serious disease. Notice the differences between the pastor's perception of his ministry as thorough and adequate, while the mother involved indicates her needs for ministry have not been met.

It came to my attention recently that Mrs. Betty Wright had expressed to a fellow Sunday School worker that she would probably not continue working with them and that their family was "looking around" for another church home. Her daughter was diagnosed as having a serious disease several weeks ago. The main reason she had given was her disappointment with the pastor because she had felt she had not been fully ministered to during this crisis. I was somewhat surprised when informed of these feelings. I had felt I had given good attention to the family based on the information I had been given previously: by telephone calls before their first trip to a distant city for tests, by an immediate lengthy visit in the home right after they returned with the bad news, and by subsequent phone contact weekly. In a home visit, her husband, Dr. Leroy Wright, a local physician, stated they were going to try to carry on a normal life-style. He indicated the daughter was going back to school, that they did not want people suddenly rushing in and hovering around and that he would let me know if there were serious developments.

I was informed of the Wrights' discontent on Saturday. On Monday I went by their home in the afternoon but found no one home. Finally, after several attempts to contact them by telephone, I was able to talk to Betty. I asked whether I might drop by to discuss the matter that had been brought to my attention. Because of the press of time during the Christmas holidays she preferred to meet several days later. I conveyed to her my apology for any neglect that had occurred and assured her of my deep concern for her family, even if it had not been strongly communicated. She responded with a positive feeling in general and began talking in terms of misunderstandings and expressed appreciation for the call.

The conversation after the holidays involved an afternoon visit at the home about an hour before the children would come in from school. I again restated my apology and affirmed to her how strongly I had been touched by the news of her daughter's illness. I stated that I wished I had been more clear in letting them know of the intensity of my empathy with them in this.

Then the crux of the conflict surfaced. What had happened was related to an earlier telephone conversation. During the first week after the hospital tests, the daughter was quite ill and unable to go to school. Betty had called me at the church during that week and conveyed to me that she had finally been able to cry and that she had really cried about her daughter. I had offered to come by her home that afternoon, but her response was, "No, just come by when you are near our house." Since she did not convey the seriousness of the daughter's illness, I did not go.

Now realizing that I had failed to pick up on her anxiety, I became aware that my apology was even more in order. After discussing her feelings about the illness, she began to express her anger toward God and toward this situation. After this there was a mellowing and she talked about her own maturing in the crisis and how she was reflecting upon her gratitude for life. I feel that the feelings between us have now been repaired.

STRESS: THE ROOT OF CONFLICT

This is not so different from experiences ministers and caring lay persons face daily. Yet, how many situations are there where the feelings of disappointment are never reported and never recognized? If you were the minister involved, would you have detected the need for immediate pastoral care? Are there ways that congregations can be taught to express openly their need for ministry? What if the Sunday School worker had not reporter her conversation to the pastor? Have you had a similar experience of needing the care of a minister, but were unable to ask for it directly? Individuals who experience grief, illness, tragedy, or the joy that accompanies marriages within the family, the birth of new children, an honor or award often assume a particular response to them from their church or minister without asking for it. Are there ways a congregation can encourage its members to request the help it needs?

Congregations may unknowingly cause other stress of which they never become aware. Ethical judgments which seems perfectly clear to the leadership of a church but have not been accepted by others on the periphery of church life may alienate those who differ. Political actions have the same effects.

A healthy congregation is one in which the stresses that are being experienced within it can be acknowledged, discussed, and appropriate action taken with respect to them. There must be some commonalty of perception about the nature of the church, its goals, its ministries, and its responses to persons in need if a management of stress is to occur. If unspoken expectations can be surfaced in a process of open communication, unrealistic hopes can be moderated before stressful situations result in a failure of the church to respond appropriately.

Unrealistic demands—Stress can result from the perception that demands are expected which are unreasonable or unrealistic. Sometimes the demands of time, money, and commitment are both reasonable and appropriate but create stress because of the guilt, apathy, or indifference of the church member who wishes a church that makes no demands. But that is not the emphasis here. Perhaps some specific examples will illustrate this point.

The church is a voluntary organization. It is dependent upon the gifts of energy, talent, and money from many people if it is to fulfill its objectives. But few congregations can function on the assumption that people will volunteer without encouragement to assume roles which must be filled. The vital church must effectively recruit individuals who will give of themselves as teachers, committee persons, and leaders. Scott Greer characterized the residents of urban neighborhoods he studied several years ago as isolates, neighboring types, and activists.[20] Greer noted the activists were those who effected change in their community—those individuals most involved in several community groups and who were themselves fully occupied in employment and family activities.

Churches have the same types of individuals. If one were to isolate the kinds of church involvement by the members of a given congregation, there would be several styles of involvement. At one end of the spectrum would be found the "inactive member." The term is itself a contradiction in terms and the reasons for it are many. Some are inactive because they have moved to another community and have not established ties in a new congregation. Some are inactive because they were never active. They joined the congregation hastily and without sincere commitment or clear understanding of their actions. Others are inactive because they were never assimilated into the life of the congregation. The full resources of the congregation were mobilized to recruit them. But once they joined, little attention was given to encouraging their full participation in its life. Among the inactive are those who were once active but have consciously chosen to be uninvolved because of personal estrangement, a life-style of sinful actions, unresolved conflict, guilt, or the feeling that they have been ignored in times of crisis. Whatever the reason for the inactivity, too few churches have taken responsibility in defining membership in such a way as to provide for the continuation of involvement as a requirement for membership. Consequently, the vitality of belonging has been eroded and the statistics on church membership for all denominations have been inflated far beyond the measure of any true meaning.[21]

A second type of church member is the "peripheral member." Such persons attend services of worship or Bible study with intermittent frequency. Regular, though limited, financial support is provided to the congregation. Such members may consider themselves deeply committed to the goals of the congregation, may be willing to accept some roles of leadership, but are seldom able to contribute significantly to the fulfillment of demanding tasks.

The third kind of member of the church belongs to the "leadership core." Such individuals are usually present at more than one half of the gathered meetings of the congregation and have been given multiple roles of leadership in the congregation. In most churches, as in most voluntary organizations, the law of common sense operates as follows, "To get a job done, find the busiest person you can to do it." So, most of the leadership of the congregations falls into the hands of those who have been prepared for leadership by an active professional, business, or community involvement. In turn, a small group of "leaders" make most of the decisions and accept most of the responsibility for the execution of the church's ministry.

Stress is often related to the formation of these groups within a congregation. A careful examination of the causes of inactivity on the part of uninvolved members may reveal that ministry at a particular stage of personal need was not performed and the individual felt unwanted within the congregation. For others their inactivity is the result of placing more demands for leadership

STRESS: THE ROOT OF CONFLICT

upon them than could be accepted. They were expected to perform without adequate nurture, encouragement, training, or recognition of overwhelming time demands.

Is it possible that the same form of stress is experienced by those most active in the congregation? Usually those who give most financially are those most involved in the processes of decision making about the direction of the church. However, there is a point of diminishing returns when the same persons are continually given new tasks. Eventually the burdens of doing more become sufficiently heavy that the leader is tempted to fail, to become inactive, or to explode in anger as a means of handling the overload of responsibilities. Consequently, it is not unusual that the illness of a key church leader affects the entire work of the congregation because it has been so dependent upon this person. Organizing church life in such a way as to involve the maximum number of people possible, simplifying the number of jobs to be done, and distributing responsibilities fairly will lower the levels of stress for church members.

Failure in management—The surest way to ensure stress for the persons of a congregation is to ask them to deal with issues which represent past failures. The old adage "failure breeds failure" is true. McGrath discovered in his review of stress research, "The experience of failure on a task is stressful in itself and has a number of effects which subsequently lead to decreased performance effectiveness."[22] Prior experience can reinforce behavior either positively or negatively.

Churches which have a history of disruptive conflict are churches which will have the greatest difficulty becoming healthy and open congregations capable of handling conflict constructively. Past failures immobilize their ability to launch innovative approaches for fear of another "fight." The following case illustrates the dynamic of feeling from individuals who have been involved in earlier conflicts.

> I have served my present congregation less than a year and one of the recurring "stories" of the past relates to harsh feeling about housing. Eight years ago the pastor refused to live in the church-owned parsonage because of its location and bought his own home. The church sold its parsonage at a loss of $7,000. Then when the pastor departed, they bought his home for a parsonage.
>
> The church has recently voted to add another full-time person to its staff. Again housing is a subject of discussion. The old feelings of what happened before are still present.
>
> I called a meeting of the board of trustees and of the building committee to present to them the situation of need for housing for the new staff member. I asked that they study the situation and recommend to the church what they felt to be the best option. As the group discussed the situation and the various options, the problem of housing

with the former pastor was raised by the chairman of the trustees. He had been chairman at the time of the previous problem. Not much was said by any of the group to his expression of concern that problems might emerge again. After an hour of open discussion about the manner in which to proceed, the meeting adjourned.

On Tuesday after the Sunday meeting the chairman of the trustees came to the church office and stated that he thought it best if he just resigned. He said that he felt he could not handle situations as he once could. I expressed my regret and affirmed his leadership and years of service. No attempt was made to get him to reconsider. He had thought the matter through and his mind was made up. He further expressed his willingness to assist in other ways in the work of the church. I thanked him for his coming and he left.

I now began to wonder about his former problem and its possible effects upon the present housing need. Several questions caused me to plan for a careful presentation of this issue so as to avoid feelings of anger or dissatisfaction. It was obvious that some people felt failure with respect to their past decisions.

Are there issues which would be difficult to discuss in your congregation because of previous controversies regarding them? Are there individuals who would have greater difficulty dealing with certain church problems because of past involvement with explosive issues which did not work out well? Remember, one of the first steps in dealing with a problem in the church is to find out how similar concerns were handled in the past.

Contradictions in the church with secular experience—A less important source of stress perhaps is the pressure that results for persons who must function in the church in contradiction to their occupational or community experience. The upper level manager of a massive corporation who routinely makes multimillion dollar decisions in the executive suite will chafe at the hour-long business meeting debating the size of the church music budget. The accountant who is a specialist at work may flinch at the uncoordinated and sloppy record systems of the congregation. The engineer, architect, or builder will often not understand the conflicts that emerge when the democratic process of the congregation places novices in the building arts on the building committee. Businessmen who function in a hierarchy of pay scales may not understand the proposal of church staff salaries that are based upon Christian principle of equality rather than status. The university dean who reviews large numbers of professional applications for employment yearly may be dismayed by the practice of pastors who refuse to show interest in the initiative of the pulpit committee he chairs when numerous friends have recommended them so highly and suggested their availability.

The Church Ministers to Stressed Persons

The first step in the management of conflict for the church is the control of

STRESS: THE ROOT OF CONFLICT

stress it places upon its members. Churches cannot control the stresses their members' experience in their homes and occupations, but they can do their best to organize themselves and to function in such a manner as to minimize the creation of additional stress for those who choose to participate in their fellowships.

The second thing the church can do in ministry to stressed persons is to take initiative toward persons who manifest their stress. What is the wise leader to do who wishes to be effective in managing conflict? To ignore the underlying stresses which affect individuals and groups is to ignore one of the basic mechanisms that triggers conflicts in the larger congregation.

One can be helped in understanding conflict if one assumes an underlying stress factor at work in every conflict situation. In such an approach there is little that one can do to prevent or anticipate conflict. But when conflict occurs, one must ask, "What are the stresses that seem to be contributing to what is happening among us?" In such a way those responsible for the decisions which must be made in the face of complex problems can better understand why a certain issue has emerged. In the face of any conflict the following questions should be asked:

1. What are the problems or issues that have given rise to this conflict?
2. Who are the groups that are involved in this given problem or issue?
3. What has happened in those groups which has brought problems or issues forward at this time?
4. What individuals within the group are most involved in the conflict?
5. What particular stresses, whether related or unrelated to the conflict, seem apparent within the lives of those individuals?
6. Has the church, or individuals within it, contributed to the stress being experienced by those involved in conflict?
7. Would an alleviation of the stresses experienced by individuals involved in the conflict diminish the conflict?
8. What options are available for lessening the stresses experienced by persons in conflict?
9. Of those available options which can the individuals and groups in conflict choose to implement as a step in resolving the conflict?

The most natural response in the face of stress is withdrawal. Yet, resolution of conflict feelings can never take place until the stresses producing them have been faced and dealt with constructively. In the following description of the encounter of the pastor of a rural congregation with the church pianist, the answers to most of the questions above can be traced in the unfolding of his experience. We are now ready to try to illustrate how the model developed in chapter 1 can be applied to real situations of ministry. We will identify the steps of the process in the margin as this case unfolds.

STEP 1
Spotting
Conflict
Potential

a. Prior
   Experience

b. External
   Stress
   Grief

   Grief

c. Internal
   Stress

   Church
   Service

   Isolation

STEP 2
Avoidance with
Integrity
Omitted
Result:
Conflict Without
Preparation

This conflict involves the pastor and the church pianist. The pianist is approximately 35 years old. She is married and has three children. She has worked hard with these children and they do a lot of singing in churches. She is a very emotional person and it appears to me that she often takes things seriously when they are not meant seriously at all. You have to be very careful in what you say around her. You never know when you might hurt her feelings, and more than likely you would not even know it. This lady will be referred to as Mrs. Rogers.

Mrs. Rogers and her family have been through a lot of troubling experiences in recent years. A few years ago (before I came) her father died. Less than two years after this a wildlife reservation was established in their area. They lived right on the borderline and the authorities refused to buy their land. Their neighbors were forced to sell and move. Even her mother had to sell and she could only watch as the house of her childhood next door was demolished.

The events leading up to Mrs. Roger's conflict with the pastor are numerous. Here are a few of the more important ones. First, it was time to get new officers for the coming year. Her position as pianist is voluntary. When asked to continue in it, she said she would have to think about it. Her mother complained to the pastor that playing was causing her a lot of anxiety, and that she felt it would be best for her daughter to quit. The church was also in the process of having a revival and the pastor was leading the singing. The conflict was brought to the surface by my reference to a clique group in the church. Many had complained to me that a few were running the church. In the sermon I said that if there was a clique, I did not know about it. I added that there was a group of faithful Christians that attended every time the doors of the church were open and that they were willing to do all they could to support the church. This happened about a week prior to the conflict.

I noticed a change in Mrs. Rogers's attitude. She responded only briefly to my attempts at conversation. The open hostility occurred after a brief rehearsal following the Friday night revival meeting.

Mrs. Rogers left the church building immediately after the rehearsal ended. I tried to stop her by calling out to her, but I was ignored. I decided to find out what the

STRESS: THE ROOT OF CONFLICT

STEP 3
Engagement
a. Open Communication

b. Feeling Response with Personal Information History

c. Anger

STEP 4
Conclusion Omitted

STEP 5
Celebration Omitted

problem was so I went out to the parking lot to talk to her. She was talking with her mother. When I asked if I could talk with her a minute, she immediately began crying. I then said I felt she had hard feelings toward me and that I would like to know so that I could correct the matter. At this point I realized I had opened a package for which I was totally unprepared.

She began, with her mother's help and encouragement, to explain what a saint her father had been and how faithful he had been to the church. She also claimed that when he died the church could have cared less. She thought the church was nice during the funeral, but after that they just forgot about what she was facing. The former pastor has spent his time with the group that I referred to as faithful Christians. She felt that they were just a clique group that wanted to run everything about the church.

She went on to explain how I had spent much of my time with this group, and that in the two years that I had been their pastor, I had only visited them on three occasions. Actually I had only been by on drop-in visits. I had never been invited to come and visit.

Many other things came out in this encounter. The focus of the matter is that she simply unloaded a lot of feelings about the church, the former pastor, the present pastor, and certain members of the congregation. I said little, but I certainly did a lot of listening.

Often the only avenue available to the leader in ministry is a reactive approach to conflict. No one is sufficiently wise to anticipate actions which will trigger conflict among fallible people. No one is sufficiently powerful to control the responses of others to remark, attitudes, actions, or feeling which inevitably trigger negative responses. Such is the lot of humankind. But surely there can be the kind of caring sensitivity within the congregations which name Jesus as Lord to explore the stresses which all of us experience as triggers of the conflict we encounter. An openness to looking at what is at work within and between participants in congregational life will provide insight into ways of working out with each other acceptable solutions to the differences we experience.

A third approach to stress ministry is to assist church members in the control of their stresses. This method of stress ministry assumes that the best approach to stress is to teach people how to recognize the stressors which affect them, how to respond to those stresses with a minimum of anxiety, and how to live life with a greater sense of control over the stressors which affect us negatively. There is presently an explosion of self-help and self-directed therapies emerging in medical and psychological circles which promise relief from stress induced illnesses, whether physical or mental. The market for such approaches is so large that a new capitalism is emerging to tap the dollars that people are willing to spend for help from any quarter. Such approaches include relaxation therapies,[23] bio-feedbacks,[24] EST,[25] Transactional Analysis,[26] and Gestalt therapy.[27] Some are helpful to such a degree for some individuals that the search for human development is constituting a new form of religion.[28] Whenever people get help for their problems, from whatever the source, that help results in a form of loyalty that has the character of religious commitment.

What is interesting about many of the contemporary approaches to stress management is that they have their counterparts in historic Christian practices which have been lost in the routines of contemporary discipleship. While most biblically-based churches preach the values of an ordered, prayerful life, too often the vitality of a consistent practice of wholeness in daily discipleship has been lost. Secular substitutes emerge when applications of historic truths become so routine as to become dull or ineffective. Why cannot congregations become the proactive agents of assisting individuals within their membership and communities to recover a sense of wholeness by becoming teachers of a disciplined prayer life? This is the Christian life-style. It is one that consists of a healthy respect for one's physical well-being (1 Cor. 6:19-20), regular meditation centering on one's daily needs in communion with the Father (Matt. 6:7-8), learning to live one day at a time (Matt. 6:25-32), balancing priorities (Matt. 6:33), a blend of care for oneself and service for others (Rom. 12:1-21), a healthy amount of regular sleep (Ps. 127:2; Eccl. 5:12), a diet that provides essential sustenance and avoids excesses (Dan. 1:6-16), and a regimen of work (Prov. 6:6-10).

A congregation is responsible for helping people live abundantly. That must include learning how to live with some management of stress. Given the conditions of modern employment, our abundance of goods and services, and the pace at which we live, the kind of life cycle described above is increasingly difficult to live. Only by deliberately making life-style decisions and consistently living by them can we expect to have healthier and happier lives. Only by developing such individuals can we expect to have healthier congregations.

The church of the future will have to become a teacher of biblical meditation amid a stressful life situation if it is to develop the kind of fellowship where conflict does not abound. The methods are innumerable and should be borrowed from any source consistent with Christian principles. What counts is that the attempt be made.

Notes:

[1] Hans Selye, *The Stress of Life* (New York: McGraw-Hill, 1956).

[2] See Daniel H. Funkenstein, Stanley H. King, and Margaret E. Drolette, *Mastery of Stress* (Cambridge: Harvard University Press, 1957); Richard S. Lazarus, *Psychological Stress and the Coping Process* (New York: McGraw-Hill, 1966); Daniel H. Carson and B. L. Driver, *An Ecological Approach to Environmental Stress* (Ann Arbor, Michigan: Mental Health Research Institute, University of Michigan, 1966); Lennart Levi, *Stress: Source, Management and Prevention, Medical and Psychological Aspects of the Stress of Everyday Life,* trans. by Patrick Hort (New York: Liveright Publishing Corporation, 1967); Sol Levine and Norman A. Scotch (eds.) *Social Stress* (Chicago: Aldine Publishing Company, 1970); Joseph E. McGrath (ed.) *Social and Psychological Factors in Stress* (New York: Holt, Rinehart and Winston, 1970); Barbara Snell Dohrenwend and Bruce P. Dohrenwend, *Conference on Stressful Life Events: Their Nature and Effects* (New York: Wiley, 1974); and Randall Collins, *Conflict Sociology: Toward an Explanatory Science* (New York: Academic Press, 1975).

[3] Gay Gaer Luce, *Body Time: Physiological Rhythms and Social Stress* (New York: Random House, 1971).

[4] Nancy E. Gross, *Living with Stress* (New York: McGraw-Hill, 1958) p. 42.

[5] Vance Packard, *A Nation of Strangers* (New York: David McKay Company, Inc., 1972) describes the multiple effects upon families and communities of the extensive geographical mobility which characterizes the United States. Many sociologists would disagree with Packard's exaggeration of the effects of moving. Sociologist Claude Fischer at the University of California in Berkeley says that the extent of mobility is declining and that positive benefits occur as a result. "A Moving Story—Is It True," *San Francisco Sunday Examiner and Chronicle,* November 7, 1976. In either case, mobility has the potential for creating stress.

[6] Gross, p. 20.

[7] Funkenstein, King and Drolette, Tables 44 and 45 and pp. 305-313.

[8] Selye, p. 266.

[9] From Thomas H. Holmes and Richard H. Rahe, "The Social Readjustment Rating Scale," *Journal of Psychosomatic Research,* 11(2):216, 1967. Used by permission of Pergamon Press.

[10] Selye, p. 32.

[11] Lazarus, p. 28.

[12] Joseph E. McGrath, "Settings, Measures, and Themes: An Integrative Review of Some Research on Social Psychological Factors in Stress," *Social and Psychological Factors in Stress,* ed. by Joseph E. McGrath (New York: Holt, Rinehart and Winston, 1970), p. 63.

[13] Gross, p. 21.

[14] Hans Selye, *Stress Without Distress* (Philadelphia: Lippincott, 1974).

[15] Ruth Stein, "Stresses That Hurt the Most," *San Francisco Chronicle,* November 9, 1976.

[16] Cf. Edgar W. Mills and John P. Koval, *Stress in the Ministry* (New York: IDOC, 1971) and Gerald J. Jud, Edgar W. Mills, Jr. and Genevieve Burch, *Ex-Pastors: Why Men Leave the Parish Ministry* (Philadelphia: Pilgrim Press, 1970).

[17] Daniel J. Levinson, et. al. *The Seasons of a Man's Life* (New York: Alfred A. Knopf, 1978) explores significant understandings of the "mid-life" crisis for American males.

[18] Every pastor and church leader should read Robert G. Kemper, "Small Issues and Massive Revelation," in *Creating An Intentional Ministry,* ed. John Biersdorf (Nashville: Abingdon, 1976), pp. 151-172.

[19] McGrath, "Settings, Measures, and Themes," p. 76.

[20] Scott Greer, *The Emerging City: Myth and Reality* (New York: Free Press of Glencoe, 1962).

[21] Lyle E. Schaller, *Assimilating New Members,* Creative Leadership Series, ed. Lyle E. Schaller (Nashville: Abingdon Press, 1978) offers suggestions of how these problems may be avoided.

[22] McGrath, "Settings, Measures, and Themes," p. 78.

[23] Relaxation therapies include a number of techniques that emphasize meditation as an approach to health. Herbert Benson, *The Relaxation Response* (New York: Avon, 1975) has written

a popular description of some of these therapies. The relaxation response involves two periods of meditation for 20 minutes each daily with four essential elements: (1) a quiet environment; (2) a mental device such as a word or a phrase which should be repeated in a specific fashion over and over again; (3) the adoption of a passive attitude; and (4) a comfortable position. Benson argues that such techniques significantly lower hypertension and ensure a healthier body. The approach is most dependent upon Transcendental Meditation but reviews other techniques such as Zen and Yoga, autogenic training, progressive relaxation, and hypnosis.

[24] Biofeedback refers to the technique of learning to control such bodily function as temperature, heart rate, and muscle tension through the recording of these functions with biofeedback machines and learning to alter them with the mind. Reduction of tension is a major goal of bio-feedback training. See Barbara B. Brown, *New Mind, New Body, Bio-Feedback: New Directions for the Mind* (New York: Bantam Books, 1974) and *Stress and the Art of Bio-Feedback* (New York: Harper and Row, 1976).

[25] EST refers to Erhard Seminars Training, a form of "assertiveness" training. Carl Frederick has described the approach to EST in *est: Playing the Game* the New Way, *The Game of Life* (New York: Dell Publishing Co., 1974). Its focus is upon individuals taking total responsibility for everything which happens to them in life by assuming a self-centered control over the events of daily life. This approach is quite selfish and manipulative. Also see Adelaide Bry, *EST: 60 Hours that Transform Your Life* (New York: Harper and Row, 1976).

[26] Transactional analysis is an approach to therapy pioneered by Eric Berne, *Games People Play: The Psychology of Human Relationships* (New York: Grove Press, 1964) which stresses the teaching of understanding how people interact with each other. Its goal is to help people live in ego states appropriate to the adult, parent or child roles of human relationships. More popular guides are Thomas A. Harris, *I'm OK—You're OK: A Practical Guide to Transactional Analysis* (New York: Harper and Row, 1969) and Muriel James, *Born to Love: Transactional Analysis in the Church* (Reading, Mass.: Addison-Wesley Publishing Co., 1973).

[27] Gestalt therapy refers to the effort to achieve "wholeness" in human relationships by integration of thinking and feeling. Frederick S. Perls, Ralph F. Hefferline and Paul Goodman, *Gestalt Therapy: Excitement and Growth in the Human Personality* (New York: Dell Publishing Co., 1951) is the primary sourcebook for this approach to therapy.

[28] See Donald Stone, "The Human Potential Movement" in *The New Religious Consciousness*, ed. by Charles Y. Glock and Robert N. Bellah (Berkeley: University of California Press, 1976) and Robert Wuthnow, *The Consciousness Reformation* (Berkeley: University of California Press, 1976).

STRESS: THE ROOT OF CONFLICT

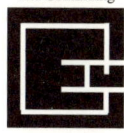

The Continuing Education Unit

Assignment

1. Describe the three stages in which the body changes in its attempt to fight the stressors it faces.

2. Here are two self-evaluation exercises to perform:
   (a) Examine Table 2-1 in order to calculate your stress situation.
   (b) Identify specific ways in which the church has created stress in your life.

3. Explain the following:
   (a) "Stress is a form of threat."
   (b) "Stress produces conflict."

4. Describe three strategies you can initiate in order to assist others in controlling their stresses.

5. Select any crisis situation you are presently facing in your church. Utilizing the 5-step model developed in chapter 1 employ this proactive approach to bring the conflict to a conclusion.

Chapter 3

Interpersonal Conflict: Everyone Needs a Referee Occasionally

Stress is quiet conflict. It may be known only to its sufferer. Intrapersonal stress may be carried in the secret recesses of one's being.

Interpersonal conflict is never private. The products of stress become visible to others when stressed individuals find themselves at odds with each other. It takes at least two to fight. When conflict surfaces in the relationships between people, it bears public results. This is the nature of interpersonal conflict.

Understanding Interpersonal Conflict

If we are to analyze the conflict interactions between individuals, we must have insight into the conditions which underlie them and may contribute to them. There are reasons for the "sparks" that ignite the fires of controversy. Becoming aware of these sparks assists in responding to them and minimizing their potential for destruction. Almost any event can become the spark which ignites conflict between persons. The quality of their relationship determines how differences are handled.

The first understanding of interpersonal conflict concerns who may be engaged in conflict. Strangers do not tend to fight with each other. One stranger may become the victim of another, but that is violence. Conflict is most likely to occur among those closest to each other. Those persons in conflict with each other who are likely to come to the attention of the church are husbands and wives whose relationship is one of growing estrangement, parents and children straining to communicate with each other, relatives whose family contests become larger than they can control, persons who work together and groups within the church who have grown sufficiently close that they can risk the openness of disagreement.

Our culture is well aware of the intimacy required for conflict. Truck drivers hum with the wail of a country singer, "You Always Hurt the One You Love."

Scholars write of the destructive impact of conflict upon families and personal relationships. Every church which has taken seriously a call to minister to hurting persons finds itself overwhelmed with opportunities for service.

Yet there is a clear potential for hurt for anyone who becomes involved in interpersonal conflict. The same closeness which allows for conflict is the closeness which can be lost in conflict. That is why grief is so often the experience of conflict ministry. A husband and wife bring their marital conflicts to a close friend in the church. After every effort for reconciliation, they conclude divorce is the most redemptive conclusion to their conflict. Now they must deal with the grief of their failures and the dissolution of their marriage. But so must their friends who have chosen to walk the dark pathway of decision with them. They must now deal with feelings of grief at their failure to work out their differences. Thus, the conflict of two persons has become the grief and concern of other individuals.

That is the calling of the conflict minister. The pain and burden of others must be accepted in part as your pain and burden. That is the grief of ministry with persons in need.[1] That is the nature of the cross-discipleship of the Christian who chooses to walk where Jesus walked.

Conflict can be healthy within these intimate relationships of trust and closeness if it is expressed without the destruction of trust. Its presence can be a sign of vitality and trust. The very presence of conflict indicates a high level of intimacy and interrelationship between the persons who are engaged in it.

This is one of the ironies of conflict. Its absence is a sign of the lack of trust, distance between persons, and an unwillingness to state feelings or issues for fear of alienating others. The task of developing healthy interpersonal relationships is then not one of stifling conflict. Rather, it is to assure that conflict takes place in an atmosphere of respect between disagreeing parties with an assurance that fairness will prevail among them.

George Bach has developed what he calls "fight therapy" for couples as an avenue for developing healthier marriages.[2] In this group approach to growth in marriage he insists that conflict within this most intimate relationship must take place according to rules of fairness which ensure each member of the marriage the right of free expression with his or her mate. Developing an avenue for disagreement within rules of fairness is one of the principal tasks of the Christian working with persons in interpersonal conflict. It is dealing with conflict at a level of integration with purpose, the goal of all conflict ministry.

Thus, the primary concern which we must have in this area is not whether there is disagreement and disorder within the lives of the people we serve, but whether there is destruction. The conflict minister must work to create a setting of mutual trust and openness where individuals and groups can deal with their differences in an attitude of Christian fairness to all concerned.

The second understanding needed for conflict ministry is interpersonal conflict provides the opportunity for personal growth. If one constantly withdraws from the arena of conflict, life will become an ever smaller circle of experiences and relationships. Only by learning how to relate to those with whom we disagree or have feelings of anger and hostility can we hope to grow in self-esteem. The persons who avoids conflict or always overpowers an opponent on an issue says to others that he or she is insecure with others. We can confront another person with our true feelings and work toward a consensus of understanding with them only when we have grown to a point of trusting the other to be open in relationship with us.

Most groups will develop toward wholeness and intimacy when they have learned to handle successfully controversial situations. How many Sunday School classes function for years with perfunctory regularity, but no joy because the participants never share themselves with each other? Much of the interaction of church groups stays on a superficial level because of the fear of honesty and the potential for disagreement which it might bring. Do not misunderstand what we are saying. We are not advocating a kind of dreary egoism which promotes maudlin confessions of feelings at every meeting of a group. What we suggest is that every group in a church has within it hurting people who need help and encouragement. If the opportunities for persons to say to each other "Please help me, I do not have all the answers" never occur, ministry will not be permitted in the very place God intended it. Weekly, thousands of adults sit in educational classes to discuss the history of a biblical passage, led by a teacher who has learned to program all feeling out of a class, assuring that no contemporary power of the Holy Spirit will ever touch their lives. Why? Habit? Fear of conflict? Lack of training? Previous distasteful experiences? Whatever may be the reasons, learning how to minister in a situation of disagreement will help most teachers develop the kind of interpersonal trust in relationships that will lead to personal growth.

Third, it must be understood that the reasons for interpersonal conflict are multiple. There are many reasons why alienation takes place between individuals. Conflict that is rooted in *attitudes* is one of these reasons. Each of us tends to assimilate a certain perspective or world view which colors the way we interpret the events we experience. So a philosophy about life, politics, economics, religion, social issues, and a host of other topics becomes internalized within each of us. The more our attitudes are shared by those around us, the more entrenched they become and the less likely conflict will emerge. But the more diverse the people with whom we associate the greater the potential for conflict and the expression of our attitudes.

This is why change stimulates conflict. Let a new pastor whose background is different from the church assume the leadership of a congregation and the old patterns of functioning will be challenged. New ways of doing things will be suggested which may result in rapid growth in the church with not only feelings of vitality but also feelings that an old way is being lost. Differences between the generations, social classes, groups of different educational levels, racial groups, and many other such factors are often the evidence of interaction between attitudinal perspectives. What must be appreciated is that the warmest of personal feelings can exist between individuals as persons and intense conflict occur because of their differences in perspective.

The classic example of this is what happens to a family during the first Christmas vacation of a child who has gone away to college. The child has been exposed to different ideas, different cultures, different life-styles, and different religious groupings from those which are primary in the family. At the dinner table the son or daughter may begin to test these new perspectives only to encounter angry and hostile parental reactions. The threat level generated by new insights further erodes the credibility of the old ways the child has learned and reinforces the values of the new. Deep animosity and even estrangement between parents and child may become the consequences of such encounters.

Emotion may trigger interpersonal conflict. This is the most difficult aspect of conflict to understand for the complexity of the human self exceeds our understanding. Interpersonal interaction is both rational and irrational, verbal and nonverbal. Words are spoken and acts are performed consciously and unconsciously which are received by others as conflictual. In Transactional Analysis there is the concept of the "crossed transaction" where an individual reacts negatively to certain actions on the part of another. Neither party may be aware of why they do not get along with one another.

All of us live with daily "crossed transactions." We often call it personality conflicts. We encounter people who bring forth anger, hostility, disappointment, or a host of other emotions for reasons we may not be able to explain. When these feelings become dominant in a marriage, business relationship, work relationship, or friendship, the help of a skilled professional may be needed to understand the reasons for those feelings—usually related to some earlier experience we have repressed in the memory of our unconscious. We are calling such help the services of a referee. A referee is one who stands outside the conflict and observes what is taking place. He also ensures that those engaged in conflict play by rules of fairness and that in their interactions the persons in conflict do not injure each other. Many will object to the use of the word *referee* to describe what often happens between therapists and their clients, pastors and church members, and children in the context of their families. We are not attempting to use the word to minimize any of the more professional functions of the caring professions. However, the word communicates some of the factors most vitally needed in a conflict ministry.

When emotional interactions are identified with persons in the church who must work closely with each other, the havoc in human hurt can be disastrous. It is often the kind of conflict that emerges between a minister and those whom he thought were closest to him in the congregation, staff members within the functioning relationship of the congregation, or friends who have exhibited close relationships with each other within the congregation.

Substantive conflict is still another kind of conflict which may be known. According to Leas and Kittlaus, this is conflict over facts, means, ends, or values.[3] In a disagreement over the facts, appropriate data can be collected to settle the issue at hand. If two persons disagree about the way a certain task should be performed, an examination of additional options may result in solutions satisfactory to both. Where people disagree about goals, a broadening of perspectives can be achieved by bring consensus. Values may be more difficult to reconcile; but if the focus of communication is confined to the values at issue and Christian teaching addresses those values, personal estrangement can be avoided.

Problems in *communication* can be a reason for conflict. In fact, improved communication is required for any kind of conflict to be engaged. All forms of conflict—attitudinal, emotional, or substantive—become more intense as a result of failures in communication. Teaching persons healthy processes of communication is both a means of preventing destructive conflict and concluding existing differences.

Reconciling Interpersonal Conflict

The goal of the conflict minister engaging interpersonal conflict is to assist those in conflict to find Christian reconciliation with each other. When reconciliation has been realized, enmity between persons becomes peace and the walls between them are broken down (Eph. 2:8-22).

The conflict ministry process can be applied to persons experiencing interpersonal conflict. In the last chapter we illustrated how stress indicators provide the signals for recognizing persons headed toward interpersonal conflict. Recognition of stress is a part of step 1: Spotting Conflict Potential.

There are other indicators of potential interpersonal conflict. Alan Filley suggests the following conditions as settings which are likely to contribute to interpersonal conflict. They are what we have called structural factors in the context of conflict in our model in chapter 1.

1. Ambiguous jurisdictions—work responsibilities have not been clarified, job descriptions written, and duplicating functions eliminated.

2. Conflict of interests—persons within the same organization must compete with each other to secure the resources to accomplish their tasks or group concerns are used by individuals in the group for personal gain.
3. Barriers in communication—pressures of time or separation of persons who need to communicate frequently with each other block interaction between persons.
4. Dependence of parties upon each other—persons cannot function by themselves but are dependent upon others to fulfill their tasks. This is often the case in closely supervised settings.
5. Complexity in organization—the greater the number of functions attempted and the greater the cooperation needed for those functions to be accomplished, the greater the risks of conflict.
6. Behavior regulations—use of standardized procedures, rules, and policies within a group which hinder effective interaction may promote conflict in a group.[4]

If a congregation has developed such structural problems, a proactive conflict ministry will call for organizational change. Much interpersonal conflict in the church can be avoided if such conditions are recognized and wise leadership is offered to effect change in the organization. Why risk the harm of irreparable fractures in relationships when a written description of committee assignments could avoid them?

The second step of our process is "Avoidance with Integrity." Avoidance of interpersonal conflict occurs by maintaining open communication within the group life of a congregation. One can characterize healthy group life in terms of a balance between high levels of trust and high levels of exposure of attitudes, information, and feelings. The group leader is responsible for developing the trust needed for high exposure.

In Figure 3-1 we have illustrated the process of growth which can occur in a group. As a group forms, it is usually low in both trust and exposure. The individuals do not know each other, nor do they know how willing they are to know each other. The bottom line in the figure illustrates where a group begins. The risk of conflict is low but the possibility of such a group accomplishing much is also low.

The first thrust toward growth for such a group must be the development of trust. This is illustrated by line 2 where the trust is high but the degree of exposure of attitudes, feelings, and information is minimal. Trust is created through the affirmation of persons in the group, developing a contract as to the goals and purposes of the group, and avoidance of judgments for expressions within the group. It is the role of the leader to monitor the group in such a way as to promote openness, acceptance, and care for each group member. The risks of conflict are low in such a group. There is usually a good

INTERPERSONAL CONFLICT

feeling between persons within it. Group life is stable. The fellowship is strong. The relationship between persons is static. We call this the stage of initiation.

The second stage is the risk stage. It requires the group to engage in exposure of the information, feelings, and attitudes within it. The third line illustrates a heightening of exposure within a setting of growing trust. Such is required if closeness in purpose and consensus in how to accomplish shared objectives are to occur. This is the most dynamic stage of group life for the risks of failure are most critical at this point.

The third level we call maturity. If the risks of exposure which exceed trust are handled by the group, trust grows, and both exposure and trust are high. Relationships grow, knowledge within the group about each others' feelings and attitudes expand, and risk lessens. It is this kind of group which is able to deal with conflict most redemptively. If, on the other hand, the group is unable to handle the exposure of the risk stage, trust lowers, the risks of mishandled conflict grow, and the group reverts to immature relationships.

A strategy of avoidance with integrity in interpersonal conflict calls for the development of mature persons in a congregation. As healthy relationships based on high levels of trust and exposure develop, conflict can be managed more openly. Where such relationships do not exist, avoidance strategies are appropriate ways to deal with interpersonal conflict until a quality of communication can be developed which will enhance trust.

Principles of open communication—Trust emerges within groups as open communication at a feeling level emerges within them. As trust grows and added exposure is realized, further trust is stimulated. A process of training in open communication within congregations is the best tactic one can employ in avoiding interpersonal conflict in the church. Consider these principles of open communication.

First, open communication is essentially dialogical. There is a two-way process of sending and receiving if communication is to occur. Too often communication is restricted to the sending aspect with inadequate attention given to how a message is received. This dialogical process has been completed when the following have taken place:

1. The communicator states his or her objective, need, or goal in clear language understandable to all of the recipients of the message. The communicator formulates a message, clearly indicating the who, what, where, and when of the communication.
2. The greater the number of ways the communication is given, the more likely it is to be understood. Variety of communication media include verbal and nonverbal messages, written messages, and symbolic messages conveyed through symbols.
3. The receiver of a message should be given the opportunity to clarify his

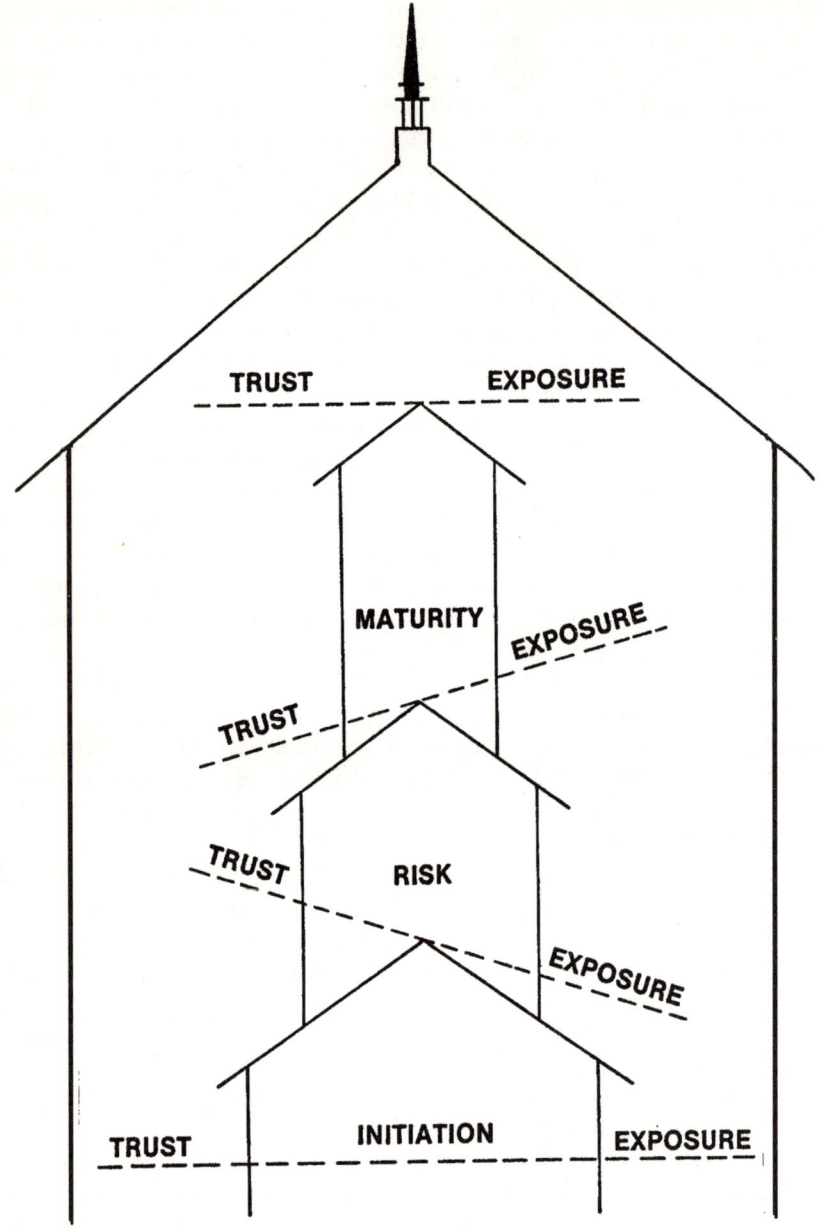

Figure 3-1: Growth Toward Balance Between Trust and Exposure

or her understanding of the communication. The sender must interact with the receiver. This is best accomplished by the receiver restating the communication received until the sender agrees it has been received accurately.
4. The communication process is complete when the receiver has made a response to the communicator. He will accept, consider further, or reject the message he has received.

Second, open communication is an expression of feeling as well as content. If there is not a congruence between the message given and the feelings which accompany the message, it will be difficult for others to receive the message. Each person in a dialogical encounter is responsible for the expression of his or her feelings. Each must accept the fact that feelings are present in every encounter whether they be love, anger, sympathy, or revulsion. Each must learn to identify the feeling present. Each must determine the focus of the feeling. What is its source? To whom should it be directed? Each person in an exchange must claim responsibility for the feelings which he or she possesses. They must be owned. No feeling is inappropriate in and of itself. Finally, each person is accountable for the appropriate expression of feeling. In some instances control of feelings will be needed. In others, their expression will be required for healthy interaction. Appropriate reporting of feeling is needed.

Feelings may shift from place to place and from group to group. Whenever conflict emerges, there is a layered effect to feelings which surfaces. In a given group you may feel respect, fear, and love toward a given person. Respect will bring forth one form of behavior, fear another, and love still another. What is important is to be able to identify to yourself which feeling has surfaced at that point in time.

Feelings can best be communicated through the use of "I" messages rather than "you" messages. "I feel _____ towards _____ and I feel _____ much" is a good way to express honest feeling. "You" messages tend to instill judgment language into a conversation. The result is mistrust and defensiveness. "You" messages are judgmental in that they communicate solutions to others' problems or depreciate them. "You" messages order, direct, command, warn, admonish, threaten, exhort, preach, moralize, advise, judge, criticize, blame, ridicule, shame, interpret, diagnose, and instruct. "I" messages give the other in communication the freedom to reject the message and assume responsibility for his or her own decisions.

In the third place, open communication allows the honest confrontation of differences between persons. We are not advocating a kind of superficial truth-telling in which persons use honesty as a banner under which to assault others or expose them before others. Rather, open communication allows expression of difference because it can be done so in a nonthreatening way. This is the "truth-telling in love" which the apostle Paul encouraged (Eph. 4:15, 25).

Honesty can best be communicated in the form of "I" messages and feeling communication. To say, "I feel what I have said was misunderstood" is quite different from saying, "You never listen to me when I talk."

Confrontation is a threatening word to many. By it we mean persons in conflict are willing to examine and discuss the differences between them. Confrontation can be done in caring ways. David Augsberger has linked the two words to speak of "care-fronting." He says: "Of the five options in conflict situations—(1) I win-you lose, (2) I want out, I'll withdraw, (3) I'll give in for good relations, (4) I'll meet you halfway, (5) I can care and confront—the last is the most effective, the most truly loving, the most growth-promoting for human relationships."[5]

If confrontation is to be healthy, anger must be controlled in the interpersonal encounter. Confrontation loses its caring dimension if accompanied by hostility and anger because both get translated into "put-down" messages. They destroy trust, bring defensiveness, and become judgmental toward others.

Productive engagement of interpersonal conflict—As you will recall, engagement of the conflict in healthy ways is the third step of our model developed in chapter 1. There are essentially three ways in which interpersonal conflict can be handled. The first, *competition,* is the most widely used form. Filley writes:

> In competitive situations there can be a victory for one party only at the cost of the opponent's total loss and the way in which the parties relate to each other is governed by a set of rules. The parties strive for goals which are mutually incompatible.[6]

Competition is a win-lose strategy of engaging conflict. Most of the conflicts settled in our culture are done so by means of competition. Athletic contests, political issues, war, challenges to authority, and the capitalist system of earning money are all built upon the principle of competition.

Likewise, most churches, especially those which function according to a congregational form of polity, resolve or perpetuate their controversies through competition. Robert's *Rules of Order* provide the guidelines whereby the differences are aired, arguments are stated on both sides of a dispute, and a vote is taken to determine the winner. Votes also determine losers. Few people like to lose. The result of such winnings and losses in the congregation is that the losers too often use their bitterness in losing as the motivation for another contest with the winner at a later time. The energies of the congregation become dissipated in warfare as the groups become crystallized into opponents and the gospel of love is clouded in the contest. The ultimate end of conflict by contest is the congregational split. Further application of this strategy will be made in the next chapter on organizational conflict.

INTERPERSONAL CONFLICT

Competition leaves a loser in every interpersonal match. No one likes to be a loser.

The second form of engagement in interpersonal relationship is *disruption*, a form of competition without the rules to play by. It is what we mean by unhealthy, dysfunctional, and growth-retarding conflict. Filley writes of disruptive approaches to conflict:

> In the disruptive conflict . . . The parties do not follow a mutually acceptable set of rules and are not primarily concerned with winning. Instead, they are intent upon reducing, defeating, harming, or driving away the opponent. The means used are expedient, and the atmosphere is one of stress, anger, or fear. In extreme cases, the parties in disruptive conflict will abandon rational behavior and behave in a manner necessary to bring about the desired outcome, the goal of defeat.[7]

Disruption is a lose-lose strategy of conflict management. By abandoning rules in the conflict process, both sides lose. There can be no winner in disruptive conflict. Personal respect for one's opponent is abandoned. Means which violate the personhood of one of God's creation are used to win. The "shouting match" determines the winner on the basis of lung power. The "fight" settles the contest on the basis of physical strength. The "murder" is settled by the strength, cunning, and weaponry of the murderer. The "sulk" may produce a winner on the basis of prowess in nonverbal communication. Many other forms of games are essentially disruptive efforts to win over one's opponent. Degrading or humiliating one's opponent in the presence of others, false accusation, gossip, humorous ridicule, and authoritarian dominance are but a few of the ways to play disruption.

Disruption leaves two losers in every such interpersonal match. There are no winners in disruptive conflict.

A third approach to conflict ministry reverses the perspective of the previous two strategies. Each of them is based upon mutually exclusive approaches to conflict. This is consistent with the definition at the outset of this book. If conflict is to be healthy, functional, and growth-producing, the approaches to ministering within it must be mutually inclusive. That is, an agreement must be sought to which both parties consent as the best possible agreement which can be achieved in that given situation. This approach Filley calls "problem-solving" which "implies the development of an outcome which provides acceptable gain to both parties."[8] We prefer to call this approach "problem ministry" in the same way we have chosen "conflict ministry" rather than "conflict resolution" or "conflict solving." There are some problems which cannot be "solved" (that is, they cannot provide the outcome desired by all parties). But every situation has within it the possibility of an outcome to which conflicting parties can agree. It may not "solve" their problem, but it does provide an avenue whereby each can do his or her part to work together on the problem. When this occurs, Christian growth has taken place.

This approach is based on what is called a win-win strategy of conflict ministry. Such a strategy seeks a consensus between parties which both can accept as gain for themselves. Thus, problem ministry seeks options which have not been thought of by those in disagreement. Further, it seeks compromises which moderate differences fairly where necessary. Where no agreements can be found, it seeks arbitration which externalizes the decision. Solomon's wisdom was recognized for his ability to suggest solutions which brought forth trust (1 Kings 3:15-28).

Whatever may be the form of conclusion—new options, compromise, or arbitration—the persons in conflict need help to bring these differences to a growth producing conclusion. We call the conflict minister who fulfills this role a referee. The referee is a neutral person who can wisely assist those in conflict in working through their conflict. Leas and Kittlaus suggest five qualifications for service as a referee.

1. He doesn't take conflict personally—difference, dislike, or disapproval do not immobilize him.
2. He has a high tolerance for ambiguity, ambivalence, and frustration.
3. He is confident in conflict management and refereeing.
4. He is not an advocate for any particular solution, nor does he take sides on the issues in this conflict.
5. He is credible to both (all) sides.[9]

Clergy are often called upon to assume referee roles in relation to interpersonal conflict in the congregation. As a pastor he or she can still take the initiative toward persons experiencing problems in ways no other professional in our society can duplicate. The pastor may still make house calls. It is appropriate for the minister to offer his services in seeking to minister to persons in need.[10]

Much of the pastoral counseling of the clergy is the performing of referee functions. Married couples seek in the pastor an impartial guide who can assist them in communication and decision making. Parents or children find in their pastor a neutral party to assist their search for happier homes. Church members who become estranged from each other look to their pastor for help. In reality most of us have had need for a referee at some time in life to lead us through conflict. Everyone needs a referee occasionally!

Informal and formal church leaders with special skill and training may serve as referees. Think of the situations which arise in every community where third-party intervention is needed for individuals to settle their conflicts.

Crisis intervention in the community can be an especially valuable referee ministry performed by the church. Where mature persons are available who fit the qualifications of referee programs of response can be developed to maintain peace between feuding neighbors, marriage partners, dating couples and relatives.[11] The clergy are often asked to use their skills in this area by community helping professions.

Unfortunately, too few ministers have been willing to employ the services of a referee in their own conflicts within their congregations. How much more healthy would be the situations of trouble between pastor and individuals if another minister, a church leader, or denominational staff person became a referee in the conflict situation helping the two parties work through their differences to a reconciled stance of Christian appreciation and love for each other. Many who have been scarred by the battles of previous forms of unhealthy conflict will object that this is simply a high ideal that will seldom be achieved. Such individuals, however, have not attempted to bring a capable and fair, third-party referee into the circle of their controversies and differences. One of the reasons for this is the feeling among many ministers that they can never admit that they might be wrong or inadequate in their personal relationships with parishioners.

Concluding interpersonal conflict.—The last step in our model is decision making. The conflict minister is not the decision maker in interpersonal encounters. The parties in conflict must decide how they will conclude their difficulties. What the minister does is to ensure that they have explored all of the potential options in the conflict, that fairness has been applied in relating to both parties, open communication has resulted and that sufficient time has been allowed for decision making. When this has been accomplished, the conflictual parties must then be held accountable for deciding how they shall conclude their differences.

In extreme situations the referee in conflict may be called upon to arbitrate a conflict that has become "stalemated." The parties are so incapacitated by their differences they cannot decide. In such a setting the referee decides the conclusion that is to be imposed upon both parties of the conflict. Such should be attempted, however, only when both parties have consented in advance to abide by the decision of the referee. When arbitration is required, a follow-up ministry of care will be needed to assist the parties not to repeat the patterns which led them into conflict.

Applying Conflict Ministry Principles

Now that we have developed our understanding of the conflict ministry process in interpersonal conflict, let us look at some specific forms of interpersonal conflict which affect churches. The following cases are real-life situations which ministers faced. Let us illustrate the process, how it was applied or not applied, in each of them.

Pastor-laity conflict—No more painful form of conflict is evident within the church than in those situations when a pastor and a church member find themselves caught in the alienation of interpersonal conflict. They may disagree over the proper method for ministry in the church, have sharp emotional clashes because of personality differences, or become angry at each other because of misunderstanding. Often one or the other of the two parties is experiencing unusual stress or anxiety and becomes unable to control the flow of emotions which hurt and alienate people.

In the following description of the encounter one pastor had with a member in his congregation the reasons for interpersonal conflict are numerous. Look for the underlying emotional differences which surface in the following case as well as the substantive points where disagreement is evident between this pastor and church member.

STEP 1
Spotting
Conflict
Potential

a. Factual Report
b. Failure in
   Structure—
   No Coordination
   of Calendar
c. Failure in
   Communuication

d. Prior
   Experience

STEP 2
Avoidance Omitted
Though
Engagement
Had Only
Win-Lose Results

STEP 3
Engagement
a. Opinion-Feeling

Mrs. Wilson is a middle-aged working mother who is director of the Senior High Sunday Department in our church. Mr. Wilson is the teacher for the boys in the same department. Their daughter is a member of the department and is graduating from high school shortly and plans to attend college. Last Sunday morning after the worship service I received a call from a parent expressing concern that a youth social was scheduled during the evening worship. The youth were to meet at the lake late in the afternoon and remain until after 9:00 PM. The social was planned as a farewell event for graduating seniors. I did not know about the social but informed the parent that I would talk to the department director about the problem.

Mrs. Wilson had a reputation for being rather temperamental and I had heard about a lot of disagreement with the former pastor and his wife. However, our relationship seemed good. We had been in their home for dinner recently and the family had been quite friendly toward us. Their daughter had participated recently in a mission trip which I had directed.

After lunch I telephoned the Wilson home and asked to speak to Mrs. Wilson. I asked about the social and we talked about the conflict with the evening worship. I stated that I thought the youth ought to be encouraged to support the regular worship services rather than plan programs conflicting with them. I also said that some parents had related this concern to me. She considered the event a church-sponsored affair which showed interest in the youth

INTERPERSONAL CONFLICT 73

b. Attitude-Conflict Without Group Involvement

c. Anger

d Retreat

e. Contradiction

STEP 4
Conclusion
a. Unilateral Decision

b. Blame

c. Anger Avoidance Omitted—can be done only in future

d. Youth Anger

Too Late—
Belongs in Step 2
a. Information Gathering
b. Seeking Referee

c. Withdrawal of Pastor

and did not think it mattered having it on a Sunday night. She said most of the kids did not come to the evening worship anyway.

The conversation did not last but a few minutes when Mrs. Wilson said I should be director of the department and hung up the telephone. Mr. Wilson called back shortly and we talked further. I tried to make clear that my opposition was not to the fellowship but with scheduling and what it said about the importance of evening worship. I would like to have attended the social myself but could not because of my commitment to the evening worship. I did not request the fellowship be canceled; I thought this would only create more trouble. The conversation ended without either of us accepting the other's reasoning.

Later in the day I met one of the teenagers downtown and he asked me rather bitterly, "What's wrong with going to the lake on Sunday?" I discovered that the fellowship had been canceled because I was against it. I went to the Wilson's home to talk to them about these new developments and the attitude displayed by the teenage boy. I got to talk to Mr. Wilson on the front porch and his attitude was, "We canceled it. I hope that pleases you." I tried to say my purpose was not to cancel a program but to point to what might be a wrong approach in our work with youth and their relationship to the church. I expressed concern that the youth had become involved in our differences and feared that our work with them might be hampered.

I shared my opinion about the incident to a few youth on an individual basis. I was told that the Sunday night time was chosen because that was the only time the Wilson's daughter was free to attend. I also talked to a deacon who is a close friend of the Wilsons and he gave me some additional insight on the personality of Mrs. Wilson. I determined from that that she accepted you as long as her plans were not disrupted. I decided to let the situation cool off. Since then I have tried to be friends with them but have not made any additional personal contacts with them.

A follow-up study on this case revealed that the conflict situation between this pastor and Mrs. Wilson did not improve. Four months later she declined to accept the invitation of her church's nominating committee to continue as the director of the department. She did, however, agree to teach the class of girls within that department. The following year she declined to teach because her younger daughter would be in the department. Two years after this incident the pastor made the following statement: "Mrs. Wilson remains very cool toward me. She usually avoids shaking my hand after worship. She comes to the evening worship only when her daughter is involved. She has also dropped out of the adult choir."

How would you analyze the conflict situation described above? Was it appropriate for the minister to initiate the conversation which he had at the time he did? Are there ways that the kind of independent scheduling by Mr. and Mrs. Wilson of a special church event could have been avoided? Does this case illustrate major problems in the total organizational life of the church? The pastor seemed to be surprised by Mrs. Wilson's reaction. Yet, when inquiring about her relationship with former pastors after the emergence of the conflict, no one else seemed to be surprised. Does this communicate anything about the pastor's depth of relationship with the Wilsons prior to the conflict? What kind of family relationship seems to be present within the circle of relationship between Mr. and Mrs. Wilson and Mrs. Wilson and her daughter? Could the pastor have avoided becoming a scapegoat for this incident in the eyes of the youth? Are there any avenues of initiative which the pastor can take to break through the barrier of apathy which now affects his relationship with Mrs. Wilson? Has the pastor's unwillingness to extend himself in relationship to the Wilsons contributed to the continued coolness between them?

Church staff conflicts—The conception of many church members is that tranquility and peace ought to exist among Christians who find themselves in roles of leadership in congregations. Yet a major cause of dissatisfaction in the ministry as well as the root of many congregational tensions are to be found within the staff of ministers who lead congregations. Often the stresses encountered by ministry leaders from within a church setting are focused upon those closest to them, families, and fellow workers, even though the roots of stress are elsewhere.

Why are there such conflicts? The reasons are legion:
- Different philosophies of how to do ministry and why
- Contrasting educational experiences regarding the appropriate role of staff members and pastors
- Varying degrees of ability and competence in the performance of tasks
- Misconceptions of authority and responsibility in the fulfillment of the church's work
- Inequitable reward and support systems resulting in envy, jealousy, and discouragement
- Personalities that do not easily interrelate

The following case is the personal account of a minister of Christian activities in a large congregation. Read the case carefully and attempt to discover his perceptions of the role of the pastor both as authority figure and as responsible for the support of those who work under that authority. Also, look for the dynamics of lay interaction that affected the interrelationship between this pastor and staff member. Most importantly, look at the issues that some would call trivial by means of which ministers must measure their self-esteem. It becomes a way to clarify to lay people that it is often in small ways that we communicate affection, support, and appreciation. The staff member who has written this case calls it "On the Chase of the Elusive Dollar."

Old First Church has a membership of about 2,400 members. There are five ministers on the staff: Senior minister, associate pastor, minister of education, minister of music, and minister of activities. Also there are a full-time children's worker and business manager. Staff salaries had just been reviewed and presented to the deacons to get ready for the financial campaign in January. During the month of December, several of us on the staff heard by the grapevine that the adjustments were near 10 percent. Since all staff members were dismissed from the deacons' meeting when salaries were discussed, we had no reliable way of verifying the rumor. However, the minister of music confirmed the rumor when he found out that his salary was to be increased by 12 percent.

STEP 1
Spotting
Conflict
Potential
a. **Shifting Roles**
b. **Unilateral Decisions—No Lay Involvement**
c. **Private, Verbal Agreements**

When I first joined the staff of the church, I did so as minister of youth, but when the church moved to its new building I changed roles and became the minister of activities. The minister of youth position was not filled. The youth program took a nose dive and, after a year, the pastor came to me and asked if I would take the youth responsibilities back along with the activities work. I did so reluctantly with the understanding that there would be extra compensation for the added work load. I was fully expecting this increase when salaries were announced in January.

STEP 2
Avoidance
Omitted by
Pastor
Event

Conflict emerged when the pastor called me to his office to tell me what my increase was going to be. It amounted to 4 1/2 percent. My reaction was one of anger, disappointment, and hurt, and I expressed this to him. He reacted that he, also, thought the increase was unfair and that he would take this up with the personnel committee. When I pressed him about when this would be done, he began to put it off. After several weeks passed

STEP 3
Engagement
a. Seeks Pastor's Support— Ignored by Him

b. Seeks Lay Support— Resisted

c. Expanding Circle of Conflict

d. Open conclusion of Interpersonal Conflict

STEP 4
Conclusion

Loss for Staff Member.

and nothing had been done, I asked him about it again. He again hedged and suggested that I talk with the members of the personnel and finance committees since this was a joint decision. I began by making an appointment with the chairman of the personnel committee. When we talked, he told me three things which led me to think that I would get no further increase: (1) He thought that the staff should be ranked pastor at the top (with the largest salary), followed by associate pastor, minister of education, minister of music, and minister of activities (with the smallest salary). (2) He also felt that the money available should go to the associate pastor to close the gap. (3) He concluded by saying that the church had paid too much to get me in the first place.

I talked with other members of the personnel committee and the chairman of the finance committee with no results. During all of this I had kept the pastor informed on the proceedings. On one occasion he informed me that one of the finance committee members, who had heard some pointed questions about my problem during the salary hearings, was rumored to be upset with me and thought I was angry with him. When I heard this I called his office and made an appointment to see him. My relationship with Don had been quite cordial and close, up until this time, and I was interested in maintaining our friendship. When I got to his office, he was very relaxed. I told him that I had heard that he was upset and he said he had heard that I was angry with him. I assured him that I was not, but that I was interested in knowing about the proceedings of the finance committee related to my salary adjustment. He said that he had asked some questions but he was not critical. Then he asked me several questions about my work and about my shifting from youth minister to activities minister. When I told him how it has been arranged and what agreements I had had with the pastor, he was surprised and said that the committee was not informed about the arrangements. He also felt that the personnel committee was unaware of these adjustments in work load. After an hour, I left feeling that everything was back to normal with Don but that I had not accomplished much in getting a further salary adjustment. However, Don did promise to be present and to support me when I met with the finance committee to discuss the matter.

When I finally did meet with the committee, Don was tied up with business and the pastor was on leave from the

Repression by Committee. Continuing Conflict

church. The committee heard me sympathetically but told me that they could not act without a recommendation from the personnel committee or the pastor. I pursued it no further.

What could have been done differently as far as the relationship of this staff member to his work setting was concerned? First, the conflict began with a breakdown in the organizational life of the church. The pastor served as this minister's supervisor, accepted responsibility for a new job role without consultation with the personnel committee, yet shifted the responsibility for compensation elsewhere. This resulted in the loss of open communication between the pastor and the staff person. No conversation needed to extend beyond the circle of the minister and the staff, had the minister involved owned his responsibility in the decision regarding a staff salary.

Second, the staff member became so emotionally involved in the issue his actions became counterproductive to a decision in his favor. His anger and frustration directed toward the pastor prevented his supporting a reconsideration of the decision. His unwillingness to accept the judgment of the personnel committee chairman ensued failure before the finance committee. While he was wise in his conclusion of personal feelings with the finance committee member, this conflict was the result of continuing to appeal a win-lose situation in which he was the loser.

Defusing anger in interpersonal conflict—As the above case illustrates, anger is one of the most prevalent results to interpersonal conflict. The pastor involved did not minister to the staff member at the point of his anger and frustration. He encouraged him to appeal a decision he was unwilling to support as pastor. He provided no interpretation of the action taken on staff salaries. He offered no defense of his failure to live up to the agreements of extra compensation for assuming greater responsibility.

All of us must wrestle with our own feelings of anger in the midst of conflict. It is a natural outgrowth of human interaction. What can be said about this monster which haunts our feelings and behavior?

First, anger is a natural and necessary feeling. Everyone feels anger, whether consciously or unconsciously. No one escapes it. One of the most helpful ministries of churches would be to help persons and families accept the reality of anger feelings without guilt.

It is interesting to note how much of the Scriptures affirm anger as an appropriate feeling. Most of the personalities of the Bible have contributed to the work of God on earth through their anger. These include Abraham, Moses, David, Jesus, Paul, Peter, and a host of others. God was often revealed to persons in history through actions of judgments as evidence of righteous anger.

There is nothing inherently wrong with feelings of anger.

Second, one is responsible for determining the source of anger. What kinds of persons or events stimulate your feelings of anger? If we can be assisted to identify our feelings, we can learn how to recognize what causes us to have them. Early childhood experiences, role models for expressing anger, and family relations contribute to learned responses for the control of anger. Personal or group counseling may be needed by individuals who find their lives maimed by the negative effects of anger.

Third, there are appropriate and inappropriate ways to express anger. The three most common misuses of anger are internalization, ventilation, and scapegoating. Internalizers get angry at themselves. Because workable ways of expressing anger have not been found, angry feelings are turned inward upon oneself. A work supervisor makes a critical comment about a persons' work. This becomes threatening. Feelings of anger surface. Fearing reprisal if the anger is expressed, the worker internalizes the feeling. Guilt about the angry feelings follows. Depression or illness may be the long-term consequences of such repeated internalization.

Ventilators of anger "lose their cool" publicly with those who are present at the time angry feelings bubble forth. With flushed face, a hostile tone, and accusatory language the ventilator explodes at what he perceives are the sources of his anger. "You have no right to say such things." "You make me angry." "You are wrong and I will not stand for it." These are typical responses. They put the responsibility for the anger upon others.

"Scapegoating" displaces one's anger upon innocents, usually those closest to us. The anger from work is displaced upon a spouse and children at home in the evening or vice versa.

While anger will be present in most interpersonal conflicts, there are appropriate ways of expressing it. The following guidelines should assist in the developing of the kind of Christian character which emphasizes a creative control of angry feelings.[12]

1. Own the feelings of anger which you have. This can best be done by the use of "I" language, rather than "you" language. "I feel very angry when I hear such things." "I am sorry but my feelings of anger become very strong when I observe this behavior." This is a style of open communication toward others with whom you feel anger. It is a way of recognizing your feelings and allowing others to know them and the impact of your relationship upon those feelings. It locates the anger where it is. It is inside us. The scriptural admonition is, "Be angry but do not sin" (Eph. 4:26a).
2. Assess the intensity of your feelings. Anger may range from mild levels of general disagreement to violent levels of rage. If the intensity of the

feeling can be determined, one's reaction can be more carefully controlled.
3. Diagnose the threat which is producing anger. Angry feelings are stimulated as a response to a threat of some kind. What is it in the tone, manner, message, or behavior of another which we perceive as threatening? If the threat can be determined, a more useful response can be made.
4. Share the perceived threat with the person from whom you feel threat. This allows a process of feedback from the other which can confirm, diffuse, or nullify the threat. "Do not let the sun go down on your anger" (Eph. 4:26b).
5. Forgive yourself and the other person involved by letting go of the anger. When such has been done in the context of Christian grace, the feelings which separate persons can be forgotten and new relationships emerge from the interaction of conflict.

When another person is the partner of the relationship who is feeling anger, the same openness in communication should be present. By affirming the feelings of another's anger, expressing the threat of that anger for you, and diagnosing the nature of the anger, new behaviors can be agreed upon which will lessen future tensions and resolve past ones. When an appropriate conclusion cannot be negotiated by the parties involved, a referee may be needed to assist the parties in concluding their differences.

Some persons live with rather high levels of angry feelings. The minister encounters such individuals in the counseling room, the committee meeting, and the hospital ward. Often the individuals are not aware of how angry they are. One very helpful ministry tool for use in counseling or group learning experiences is the "Inventory of Anger Communications" by Millard J. Bienvenu, Sr. [13] By taking the inventory, individuals can begin to identify the areas of personal growth which are needed for more productive conflict encounters.

Finally, learn to put anger into a theological perspective. Augsburger suggests four personal understandings about anger which are related to a sense of identity as a child of God:

> I can be aware of my feelings of anger. (I am accepted.)
> I can own my resentments, my hate, my hostility. (I am loved.)
> I can discover new says of experiencing my negative and my positive feelings. (I am free to grow.)
> I can be angry in creative, loving, caring ways. (I see it modeled in Jesus.) [14]

Christian discipleship requires of the body of Christ a higher standard of behavior. While both conflict and anger are natural, there are disciplined ways they can be exercised. This is a priority the church must never forget.

In this chapter we have sought to apply some of the understandings of Christian ministry as they relate to interpersonal conflict. If they can be utilized, congregations can be more loving and caring. Our world will be healthier as a result.

The concerns of conflict ministry grow ever larger as the model we have developed is applied. Now that we have seen insights concerning conflict between persons, let us examine its impact upon churches as organizations.

Notes:

[1] James E. Dittes, *When People Say No: Conflict and the Call to Ministry* (San Francisco: Harper and Row, 1979), pp. 1-9.

[2] George R. Bach and Peter Wyden, *The Intimate Enemy: How to Fight Fair in Love and Marriage* (Caldwell, NJ: Morrow, 1969).

[3] Speed B. Leas and Paul L. Kittlaus, *Church Fights: Managing Conflict in the Local Church* (Philadelphia: The Westminster Press, 1973), pp. 31-35.

[4] Alan L. Filley, *Interpersonal Conflict Resolution* (Glenview, Ill: Scott, Foresman and Co., 1975), pp. 7 ff.

[5] David W. Augsburger, *Caring Enough to Confront* (Glendale, CA: Regal Books, 1973), p. 11.

[6] Filley, p. 2.

[7] *Ibid.*, pp. 2-3

[8] *Ibid.*, p. 3.

[9] Leas and Kittlaus, pp. 65-67.

[10] See Wayne E. Oates, *Pastoral Counseling* (Philadelphia: The Westminster Press, 1974), pp. 120-142, and Paul Mickey, Gary Gamble, with Paula Gilbert, *Pastoral Assertiveness* (Nashville: Abingdon, 1978).

[11] Gerald A. Specter and William L. Clairborn (eds.) *Crisis Intervention* (New York: Behavioral Publications, 1973). This book explores many facets of community-based crisis intervention programs.

[12] These guidelines have been adapted from suggestions in John E. Jones and Anthony G. Banet, Jr., "Dealing with Anger," *The 1976 Handbook for Group Facilitators,* ed. by J. William Pfeiffer and John E. Jones (Lojolla, CA: University Associates, Inc., 1976), pp. 111-113.

[13] See *The 1976 Handbook for Group Facilitators,* pp. 79-85.

[14] Augsburger, p. 44.

INTERPERSONAL CONFLICT

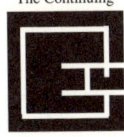

The Continuing
Education Unit •

Assignment

1. Differentiate between "interpersonal" and "intrapersonal" conflict.

2. Explain how withdrawal from conflict can inhibit the opportunity for personal growth.

3. Analyze the most recent incident of conflict either in your church or in your interpersonal relationships.
   (a) Was the reason emotional, substantive or a problem in communication?
   (b) What method of engagement did you employ to bring the matter to conclusion?
   (c) What would you do differently?

4. You are a group leader. Explain in detail how you would go about developing trust within the group.

5. Explain the difference between an "I" message and a "you" message. How does this understanding relate to managing conflict?

6. Using the Leas/Kittlaus set of qualifications evaluate your effectiveness as a referee.

7. The authors cite two case studies, "pastor-laity conflict" and "on the case of the elusive dollar." On pages 74 and 77 they set forth a series of questions. Write out your responses to each one.

8. Identify a situation in which a church member responded inappropriately in anger. Did the person internalize, ventilate or "scapegoat"? Outline a strategy that would help such a person to let go of the anger.

Chapter 4

Congregational Fights: Organizational and Community Conflicts

Stress is the reality of intrapersonal conflict suffered in the inner recesses of one's being. Interpersonal conflict is the contest between persons which erupts between individuals. Both may be private forms of struggle with which the minister wrestles behind the closed doors of pastoral office or parishioner's home.

There is no privacy, however, for the minister who must deal with conflicts which invade the group life of the Christian congregation. Committee meetings, Sunday School classes, small-group gatherings, congregational business sessions, and community controversies are too often the forum for expressions of conflict which become hurtful to meaningful fellowship.

Organizational conflict is as real in the church as in any human institution. It is often dealt with less openly in the church, however, because of a basic feeling among many that disagreements and differences ought not occur among Christians. This understanding of the church in its humanness results in the desertion of many members in the face of ripples of differences which spread through all congregations.

The purpose of this chapter is to provide principles and guidelines for understanding the ministry of management in congregational structures as it relates to internal or external conflict. Much conflict results from poor leadership, poor planning, and poorly implemented plans within the church. It is our assumption that the first priority of conflict ministry in the church is the exercise of thoughtful, caring ministry to individuals experiencing stress and interpersonal conflict.

The second priority ought to be an equal concern for the church as a structure. The creation of good structures, workable means of communication within them, and emotionally shared processes of decision making will result in a community within which conflict can be healthy and growth producing.

James D. Anderson and Ezra Earl Jones suggest there are four components in church life which require ministry. These are purpose, organization, leadership, and community.[1] Mismanagement of any one of these can result in dysfunctional conflict, the loss of congregational vitality, and an exodus of members. Focus will be given in this chapter to conflict as it relates to the components of organization and leadership. In this way the internal and external dimensions of congregational life can be examined.

The Values of Organizational Conflict
Conflict is a neutral word. It is a descriptive term which speaks of differences unresolved and disagreements unsettled. While many assume differences and disagreements are to be avoided, it is our assumption that they cannot be avoided. What should be analyzed are the consequences of conflict, not conflict itself. While conflict itself has no moral value per se, the results of church conflict may be healthy or unhealthy, functional or dysfunctional, positive or negative.

Positive values—Many of the products of conflict are positive. Personal growth occurs as persons learn to identify their differences, develop mutual understanding of them, and seek compatible alternatives for resolving them. Churches mature as the individuals within them learn to express their feelings, dissatisfactions, and concerns to find an open willingness to be heard and supported by fellow Christians. Families develop intimacy as each member learns how to engage constructively in conflict.

The first positive benefit of conflict is identity. It forces persons to "choose this day whom you will serve" (Josh. 24:15). Substantive issues which confront congregations force them to decide on their understanding of the mind of God in earthly affairs. Every situation of conflict carries with it the underlying theological question. "What does it mean to be the people of God in this situation?" How congregations answer that question determines their continuing purpose as a local church. The more clearly the purpose of a congregation is stated, understood, and emotionally affirmed by its membership, the more likely its response to issues within it will be consistent. Conflict in the early church over the question of whether Gentiles had to be circumcised to become Christians, and thus become Jews, forced the Jerusalem council to choose a universal understanding of the Christian faith (Acts 15:1-29). This one decision shaped the missionary character of Christianity though its implementation resulted in continuing conflict.

Conflict within congregations over substantive issues of theology, ethics, politics, or organizational style often led to numerical multiplication through division. How ironic that the congregation which divides over a substantive issue often becomes two congregations, each of which is larger than the original congregation. Anytime a religious group is diffused in its self-identity, it risks the potential of the winnowing process of finding itself through conflict.

Dean Kelley has documented the importance of identity in church growth.[2] Interestingly, the groups he catalogs as the fastest growing are often conflict laden and schismatic in their history. They have grown as conflicts forced them into more sharply defined identities of purpose and function.

A second result of conflict is power. The absence of conflict within a group is often the indication of the presence of powerless groups within it. They are like the couple who has a perfectly peaceful marriage because the wife always does whatever the husband wishes. Her needs are never met nor her wishes ever voiced!

Conflict can be the means for silent and uninvolved groups to become a part of the church by active participation in the decisions of the congregation. The church which asserts itself in the face of community crises gains respect and power from its involvement. A persecuted minority gains power by its refusal to abdicate to the pressures for conformity to majority wishes. And in contests where the rules are clear to both parties, conflict allows a winner to be declared and the contest to be ended. This occurred in the Circle City Church over the issue of changes in leadership. For years the same men served for life as deacons. Sunday School teachers and church officers were seldom rotated. Then a new power plant was constructed within three miles of the church and new families moved in. Younger adults joined the church and began offering to serve in leadership roles. The old-timers were threatened and resisted. Finally, the pastor led the church to write a set of bylaws which the church never had before. They proposed a method of rotating leaders. For four months the changes were discussed. Everyone agreed no vote would be taken until every question about the change had been discussed openly. At least two thirds of the members would have to approve the changes for them to be accepted. When the vote was taken, the bylaws were approved by a vote of 120 for and 40 against. But those who were outvoted supported the decision because they had agreed to the rules and were committed to the church decision. Some new leaders were elected, additional growth continue, and a new sense of mission accompanied the changes in the church. The church became stronger as a result of facing conflict.

Power for some one or group is inevitable where there is controversy. Where organizations are structured for win-win forms of decision making, everyone gains power by making decisions. The synergistic effect of one plus one equals three begins to operate as congregations live out of their purpose to act with consensus on the issues confronting them. Their mission under God becomes realized through the victory of a common purpose being realized in their midst. For the church the presence of God becomes real to its members, and a sense of excitement pervades the atmosphere of its common life. In turn, its spirit becomes contagious as others are attracted to the spirit of relationship which is observable in the church. Victory is experienced as the power of God's Spirit at work among his people.

The third positive value of conflict is group solidarity. Groups which are threatened by conflict develop a solidarity with each other and become loyal to their cause. Group solidarity will be especially strong if the conflict is external to the organization and threatens its existence.

Threat, whether personal or social, is one of the most powerful environmental factors shaping our lives. In the face of threat persons will turn inward for the psychological defense mechanism needed to cope; or, they will move toward each other for support in the face of crisis. Dean Hoge has documented in his research that the degree of perceived social threat is a major factor influencing whether church members are basically private or public in their faith orientation.[3] Church members who experience the threat of anxiety or anger in the church begin the process of retreat from participation in its life unless supported by others.[4]

The recognition of this reality has often been used consciously or unconsciously by those who build the solidarity of the church by offering themselves as a protection against threat. Demagogic pastors often stimulate the feelings of anxiety in their community and offer their church as a haven of security. The threat of Communism, encroaching denominational power, the so-called liberalism of educational institutions, or the power of government have all been offered as external enemies from which the church must protect itself. The demagogue knows that an external enemy is the best protection one has against personal questions of authoritarian power.

A fourth value of conflict is perseverance. A group engaged in a conflict which it believes is worth a struggle is a preserving group. This is especially true of minorities who feel strongly about their cause and face resistance. For some it is the perception of need for change within a church which gives to them a sense of participation in its life.

Another positive dimension of conflict is its diffusion of more serious conflict.[5] The openness of a congregation to maximum participation in decision making allows for differences to become resolved before emotionally laden factions emerge into destructive elements. Organizations, like a pressure cooker, must have release valves or the "lid will get blown off." Ministry to persons experiencing genuine conflict is the release valve for more intense and more potentially destructive conflict.

Finally, conflict results in the search for more creative and satisfying feelings and solutions. The pressures created in personal relationships allow for the challenging search for new information, more adequately descriptive facts, new alternatives, and different organizational arrangements. The discovery of the new is rooted in the inadequacies of the old. Without conflict there is no creativity. Edward B. Lindaman suggests that new discoveries rest upon new perceptions of reality. He writes:

> What seems mundane and trivial is the very stuff that discovery is made of. The only difference is our perspective, our readiness to put the pieces together in an entirely new way and to see patterns where only shadows appeared just a moment before.[6]

Negative values—The negative dimensions of conflict are most real to those who work in the church. Most church leaders bear the emotional and spiritual scars of mishandled controversies. They are often the recipients of the negative remarks, aggressive behavior, and occasional violent actions from those who are insensitive or uncontrolled. It is little wonder that so many conflicts are feared when one can document unhealthy conflict experiences in churches among clergy and laity alike.

Personal hurt is the most obvious negative result. Wounds are inflicted into the psyche of persons when controversy or disagreements degenerate. There are no guarantees that any conflict situation will not become dysfunctional and harmful. That is the risk of conflict ministry.

What must be recognized is that there are different kinds of pain in conflict. Personal hurt occurs when conflict becomes personalized and laden with emotion. Leaders may not be able to create the kind of community where differences can be aired without attack and harm. An important dimension of ministry in this area is to provide the kind of preaching, teaching, training, and relationship that will allow open discussion without abuse. Much of the apostle Paul's correspondence dealt with the pain of conflict. He had been the recipient of abuse (2 Cor. 9:8-12; 11:16-29; Phil. 1:12-13). At times he was harsh in his judgments of others (Phil. 3:2; 1 Cor. 5:1-5). But he saw clearly that a purpose and the presence of God could be found in even the negative experiences of pain and hurt (Rom. 8:31-39). He was ever admonishing the young Christians of churches he served to settle their differences in reconciliation (Phil. 4:2-3). Much of his writing addresses the practical issues of conflict within families (Eph. 5:21 to 6:4; Col. 3:18-21), in relations with those outside the church (1 Cor. 5:9-13), and especially relations between Christians.

When the wound of hurt has been inflicted, however, another form of hurt must be brought to bear. That is the pain of healing. The natural inclinations are to withdraw, soothe over, or ignore the hurt which has occurred. Wounds untended become infected, which, if continually ignored, eventually require surgery.

The metaphor is equally true in human relationships. Broken relationships fostered by unhealthy conflict begin a process of estrangement which grows if reconciliation does not occur. Savage documented in his research that conflict with a pastor, family member, or a fellow church member were the major events leading too inactivity in the church.[7] Inactive members begin an initial withdrawal at the time of conflict. They move gradually away from the church. When the community of faith does not respond to the pain experienced, total withdrawal from the church results.[8] Paul recognized this principle in telling the Philippian church to help Euodia and Syntyche settle their differences.

A second negative value of conflict is the possibility of rigid structures. The formation of rigid processes for handling future issues is usually the by-product of dysfunctional conflict. Churches which have experienced intense controversy often become so frozen that much energy is directed toward the suppression of conflictual feelings or actions. Rules and regulations are written to govern group life. Vitality is lost. The church becomes a place of inactivity.

A related consequence of conflict is the dissipation of energies into nonproductive goals. While it is true that high levels of energy can be maintained in conflict settings, energy is used for goals that result in little purpose as far as the mission of the church is concerned. A close examination of many conflicts reveals struggles over issues that are insignificant in any ultimate sense. The smaller the organization, the more likely the issues fought over will be minor. Recorded in the minutes of one rural Kentucky church is a church division into two congregations. The issue? Disagreement over which side of the sanctuary to locate the church piano! Some conflicts are not worth the energy they use.

Guidelines for Organizational Conflict in the Church

Conflict ministry is quite situational. How one guides the process of congregational decision making depends upon many factors. The size of a congregation, its history, the nature of specific issues confronting it, and community change all affect the actions to be taken in ministry.

Any meaningful set of guidelines must recognize the dual nature of religious communities. A church is both a fellowship of people and an organization. Anderson and Jones call this the associational and bureaucratic natures of the church.[9] As a fellowship, the congregation functions on the basis of opinions, values, and relationships which exist between people. Any process of ministry requires a common agreement by those involved if they are to give their continuing voluntary support to church action. The more a church functions as a fellowship, the more necessary are consensus-type actions required of the group.

As churches grow in size and complexity, their character becomes increasingly bureaucratic. The first step in that process is the addition of professional staff leadership. Most congregations smaller than 250 resident members will have only one full-time, paid professional in a role of leadership—the pastor. As churches exceed that size, they will, of necessity, expand the paid leadership, develop a system for a division of labor, and become increasingly dependent upon professional leaders for guidance in the direction of ministry.

Two assumptions are made in the following guidelines. First, we make the theological assumption that the character of the church as the people of God living in relationship with the Father of our Lord Jesus Christ and each other is a living fellowship. Faith is relational.

The second assumption we make is a sociological one. Complex organizations can be structured to maximize their associational rather than their bureaucratic character. This is not to deny that bureaucracies can be efficient and effective. Rather, it is to assert that the purpose of an organization will determine the character of how it is structured. Highly efficient managerial processes which work exceedingly well in profit-making, product-producing corporations are often conflict producing in church settings. A relational and people-oriented group must develop structures consistent with such a purpose.

Develop win-win structures—The best strategy for organizational conflict ministry is preventive—develop structures which function on the basis of win-win approaches to decision making. Traditional church politics are built upon win-lose strategies for action. The typical congregation, in our experience, pursues the following procedure:

1. A series of standing or ad hoc committees are elected by a board or congregation as the originating body for new policies, new ministries, or implementing existing church programs.
2. Membership on these committees is often designed to be representative of the church and consists of those who will allow themselves to be elected. Those best known and most visible in congregational life get elected.
3. Committee actions are made by majority vote. Changes in existing approaches require referral to a council, an elite group such as deacons or elders, or to the congregation. Each of these groups accepts or rejects the committee's work by majority vote. Consequently, the final arbitrating authority is a different group from those persons most familiar with the issues at stake in change. A majority on an important committee decision may become a minority in the larger forum.

This system works very well as long as there are neither unsettling nor controversial questions about the actions of any committee in the church. It is a procedure that can move swiftly through the channels of decision. However, it becomes a totally unworkable structure any time there is an emotional issue over which a substantive minority are willing to fight. Issues which begin as clear consensus decisions at the committee stage often become win-lose contests at a council or congregational level.

A case in point concerns the experience of Old Second Church in its decision about its future. Follow again the conflict ministry process in the left-hand margin.

STEP 1
Spotting
Conflict
Potential

a. **Prior History**

b. **Change**

c. **Planning**

This church meets for worship in a building located in the downtown section of a city of about 40,000 population. The sanctuary was built in 1887. About seven years ago the church elected a long-range planning committee to study the needs of the church and the possibility of a building program. The committee reported their findings and encouraged the church to take steps toward a new building. Nothing more was done at that time.

The present pastor came to this church three years ago. Interest began to mount toward a building program. The pastor, with advice from a special deacon's committee, appointed a building study and planning committee. The church gave approval by formal election. They made a thorough study of the needs of this church for a building program in the light of changing conditions in the community. All information gathered pointed toward a transition in the community within ten to fifteen years. It was noted, in fact, that the process of transition from residential to commercial already was taking place. Parking was limited and additional property near the church was not available.

The pastor was involved directly with the proposed building program from the beginning, taking a firm leadership role. It was the hope of all concerned that a building program would go through with minimal discord. The pastor and committee began to anticipate difficulty, however, when they turned toward the idea of relocation. The pastor did not push in this direction; but he and the committee became convinced it was the most feasible move.

As the building study and planning committee began looking toward the possibility of relocation, available property was found a mile from the church. A survey revealed 80 percent of the resident membership lived outside the immediate church community. The relocation site would be conveniently accessible to most members. It would be nearer to 50 percent of the membership and just as close to many others. About 30 percent would have to travel a mile further.

d. Closed
   Communication

Informal
Communication—
Rumor?

e. Inadequate
   Time

STEP 2
Avoidance with
Integrity Omitted,
When Potential for
Conflict Was Noted.
At Least Three
Hearings Were
Needed.

STEP 3
Engagement
a. Forcing

Event #1
b. Avoidance Omitted
 a Second Time—
   No Feedback
c. Official Approval
   to Continue is
   Needed

Event #2

Avoidance Attempted

Advisory personnel from the denomination's church architecture department were brought in. The local area planning commission also was consulted. Each one, acting independently of the other, advised the church to relocate. A price had been set on the proposed site, and the Church Architecture Department gave an approximate size and cost of an auditorium and education building. A local architect confirmed this estimate.

The committee made periodic reports to the church, saying that progress on the study was being made and that advisory personnel were being consulted. Nothing definite about relocation was revealed to the church during this time. As the time neared for the full report to come to the church, much anticipation was prevalent in the membership. The committee decided to propose relocating. The pastor gave full support to the decision.

The committee prepared a written report to give to all the membership. It met first with the fellowship of deacons and made a full report to them. The deacons gave their support to bring it before the church. The committee made its report to the church on a Sunday morning. A business session was set about two weeks later, on a Wednesday evening, for discussion of the proposal. All aspects of the proposal were discussed freely. A good spirit prevailed but strong opposition was apparent. The committee recommended that the church sell the existing property and building, purchase the proposed site, and build new facilities. It further proposed that two-thirds majority be required for the move to pass. The vote was taken by secret ballot on a Sunday morning after the worship service. The result showed 55 percent favoring relocation and 45 percent opposing.

Since the original move did not receive the required two-thirds vote, the committee regrouped to decide what to do next. It was thought that many would favor building on the present site. A proposal to buy additional property adjoining the church was also defeated. The committee members decided they had gone as far as they could, so they resigned.

Last September one of the deacons made a motion for the church to vote again on purchasing the proposed site for relocation. The pastor had talked with him and others about the serious conflict which might develop; but he insisted, feeling certain many others felt as he did. Another

Event #3

**STEP 4
Conclusion—
Continuing Conflict**

No Celebration

No Growth

time was set for discussion, and the vote was taken on a Sunday morning by secret ballot. Only this time, a simple majority was to carry the motion. It passed by a narrow margin.

A serious conflict developed between those who favored relocation and those who opposed. Having been previously identified with the proposal, the pastor was right in the middle of the controversy. Tension exists at the present time as the church awaits a report from the trustees on the relocation site. A year of time having passed, a further complication has developed. There is a strong possibility the property will not now be available. Many of the older people are greatly upset. Their resistance to the change is strong. The pastor feels deeply with these members, and he questions the advisability of following through under these conditions.

The pastor has had difficulty throughout this venture trying to promote unity and at the same time keeping the church moving toward a much needed building program. He has been effective to some extent by keeping communication open with both groups. He was successful in maintaining order in potentially explosive business meetings. The pastor would advise the committee to report more fully to the church from the beginning, if the process could be done again.

Here is a democratic system at work that did not work. All had an equal voice in the processes of deciding, but no votes have more power in situations of conflict than yes votes. Everyone in this congregation became losers, for the church lost its vitality by becoming embroiled in continuing conflict. Win-lose methods often result in lose-lose realities. Filley suggests the following common characteristics of the two:

1. There is a clear we-they distinction between the parties, rather than a we-versus-the-problem orientation.
2. Energies are directed toward the other party in an atmosphere of total victory or total defeat.
3. Each party sees the issue only from its own point of view, rather than defining the problem in terms of mutual needs.
4. The emphasis in the process is upon attainment of a solution, rather than upon a definition of goals, values, or motives to be attained with the solution.
5. Conflicts are personalized rather than depersonalized via an objective focus on facts and issues.

6. There is no differentiation of conflict-resolving activities from other group processes nor is there a planned sequence of those activities.
7. The parties are conflict-oriented, emphasizing the immediate disagreement, rather than relationship-oriented, emphasizing the long-term effect of their differences and how they are resolved.[10]

Any method which decides a winner and a loser can become a lose-lose process. Majority vote, appeal to authorities, compromise, and resorting to rules are forms of settling issues without a genuine solution to the problem at hand.

How can a win-win strategy be developed? First, a church must have a consensus as a fellowship about its reason for being. Unless there can be agreement about the basic purpose and specific goals, there can be little unanimity when the church acts in ministry. Management specialists Jane and Rensis Likert call this beginning point "integrative goals."[11] It is finding the glue which holds a church together.

It is likely that many leaders will consider this point superficially obvious. But it is not. The mobility of the contemporary American community is such that one can no longer assume a consensus of values, beliefs, or expectations regarding the church! Approximately one half of the population change their residential addresses within a five-year period. To the degree a congregation is effective in ministry to mobile Americans,[12] it must assume responsibility for fostering an acceptance of church goals by newcomers or continually involve nonmobile members in reassessments of their mission in the light of changing needs.

Second, a church becomes a win-win congregation if it can learn to depersonalize the issues before it. Opinions and facts cannot be identified with the personal character of those espousing them. The pastoral leader has a major role to play in focusing upon the contributions of each member. He or she must begin by deemphasizing status or authority of the leaders. If the leader is competitive and strives to use the group for gain, individuals will compete for leadership. If the leader can foster a sense of group equality, individual contributions need not be attacked and "put down." The gathering of facts, the identification of individual suggestions as "our" ideas, and the use of referees to moderate differences can keep the process on an objective level.[13] Notice how personally committed to one choice both the pastor and committee became in the case above.

Still another strategy in the development in win-win church life is to train persons in the processes of conflict skills. People can learn how to manage their differences more skillfully if they have opportunities to do so in conflict-free settings. Workshops in conflict skills, active listening, dynamics of group life, decision making or simulation games of conflict can be excellent means for helping a church learn the process of associational life. How ironic that we place such high expectations for healthy personal relations with so little training in how to achieve them! The congregation which wishes to minister effectively to persons is one which plans for training experiences which will help it cope with its struggles.

Fourth, a win-win congregation takes advantage of the resources of outside specialists as it plans its life. Open congregations expose themselves willingly to outsiders who have the gifts to provide specialized leadership. A consultant in planning, decision making, or information-gathering about potential ministries can assist the congregation at the point of process. A healthy congregation will seek the counsel of appropriate consultants when it finds itself becoming conflictual. In some settings a referee may be needed to assist in facilitating a new direction when win-win commitments weaken and become competitive struggles. Notice how Old Second Church utilized outside consultants. Their insights and advice were sought as the study committee explored options, but their recommendations were not shared with the wider constituency of decision makers early in the process.

Finally, the win-win congregation becomes as concerned with process as it is with product or results. How a church decides an issue becomes as important as what it decides. This principle of church life rests upon a theological assumption about the character of a church. If it is to reflect the character of the Christ it claims to follow, a church's actions must flow from its being. If disciples of Jesus Christ are excluded from the decisions which affect their lives, it becomes difficult for them to feel they are a part of the body which reflects His character.

Employ open processes in decision making—If process is so important, can a congregation ever decide anything? Yes, for the process of healthy decision making brings the group to a search for the best alternative for its situation. Let us review the process through which a good congregational decision should flow. We are assuming that the decision is a major one in which the whole body should participate.

There are three components of the decision-making process: preparation, decision, and conclusion. Each is important in conflict ministry. The steps of preparation have been outlined below.

The decision-making process begins with a general commitment to make a decision regarding future goals, an issue at hand, or a specific conflict. Many conflicts emerge because there is no desire to decide for a change. The minister, a small group within the church, or dissident individuals often push for changes which are defeated by the whole group. Effective decision-making processes begin with a commitment of the congregation to utilize the decision-making process. The decision to appoint a planning committee, building committee, or social action committee becomes a congregational commitment to participate in a later substantive decision.

Stage 1
Preparation
Group Commitment to a Decision
Collect and Analyze Data
Explore Alternatives
Seek Feedback to Alternatives
Identify New Alternatives

Figure 4-1
Flow of Preparation in Decision-Making Process

There are a wide variety of opinions about the composition of such committees. Some leaders will emphasize the need for a representative committee, others of specialists in the matter at hand. It may be important to select persons who are trusted by the congregation so that effective convincing can be done when the group's work is completed. The major criterion ought to be function. The nature of the committee's work ought to determine its membership. Those persons most interested, most skilled, and most willing to commit their time to the work of the committee should be chosen. The chairperson, on the other hand, should be one who understands how to lead a group through a decision. He or she should also have an intimate knowledge of the larger congregation, be trusted by it, and able to provide an effective communicative link with the congregation.

If you will recall the case of Old Second Church, it is apparent this step was omitted. The pastor was the moving force in the establishment of a building committee. The congregation satisfied his desire, but there is no evidence that it was committed to making a decision that would result in substantive change. Further, the committee chosen did not become a communicative link with the larger group.

The second preparatory step is to collect and analyze all pertinent information. It is at this point that the process often breaks down. Some church groups have never been trained how to gather information about their church or community. Yet a decision can be only as good as the data upon which it is based. This is the most time-consuming part of decision making. Too many groups fail at this point because those chosen for this task are core leaders who are busy within and outside the church. They find this task overwhelming and frustrating.

An outside consultant can be a valuable resource at this point. Bringing a specialist in from the denominational office, community, or a national group with expertise in the issue, can often facilitate the speed at which a group can work.

When the information has been gathered, analyze its significance in relation to the decision at hand. Discard useless data and put into writing a summary of your findings.

Third, explore all of the possible alternative decisions which could be made in light of the information gathered. Alternatives are often listed only in terms of the ideals of what might be desired. An alternative should be stated in terms of four aspects. How much *time* will be required to complete this chosen alternative? What will it *cost* in dollars and the participation of people to implement? What will be the *probable results* for the church if this alternative is chosen? How will these results *affect the community* in which we are located? Write out each of the alternative decisions which could be made, including time factor, costs in money and personnel, and probable results for the church and community.

Fourth, involve the larger decision-making group in the feedback process concerning selected alternatives. Groups that are intent on making win-win decisions will involve the larger group at this stage of decision making. Circulate to the group the information which the committee has gathered along with the set of alternative decisions which are being explored. Establish a formal process where congregational members can communicate their preferences among alternatives or additional information the subgroup may have overlooked. Where the potential for conflict is high within a group, it is especially important that all persons have equal access to the information collected, the alternatives considered, and the feedback process. If the building committee of Old Second Church had done this, it would have encountered a different set of dynamics in its decision-making process.

Fifth, identify any new alternatives which emerge from the feedback process and select one alternative from the list of options for the recommendation to the congregation. The selected alternative should be viewed as the best possible option given that church's needs and mission. Caution must be exercised not to ascribe too much value or authority to this alternative. Do not over promise the results of the decision. Too often single decisions are viewed as "the solution to all of our problems." In a real sense, no decision solves problems. It is the choice of what problems with which you will live. It is the selection of a given set of consequences which are likely but never certain.

Stage 2
Making the Decision
Agree on the Rules (Procedures for Deciding)
Allow Sufficient Time

Figure 4-2: Elements of Decision Making

The congregation is ready to finalize a major decision when the facts have been gathered and a priority alternative has been selected from among the available options. Several matters of concern need attention at this stage of the process.

First, agree on the rules of decision making. The best win-win method for decision making is consensus. Most churches function with two methods of deciding. They have a formal process of voting with a majority required to approve an action. Then there is an informal understanding that any action which has a large minority of opposition cannot really be implemented. Seldom would a wise minister accept the invitation of a congregation to serve as its pastor with a call vote of 52 percent! Nor would one wish to proceed with construction of a social service building in the community if one third of the congregation vigorously opposed it. A one-third negative vote will nullify a two-thirds positive vote. The more a church functions as a fellowship of people, the more nearly a minority of folks rules its common life if governed by voting.

We suggest that consensus styles of rules be adopted by congregations as the form of decision making. The parliamentary procedures of Roberts' *Rules of Order* are effective as win-lose rules for they make the most skillful parliamentarian the winner. The group is the winner when consensus is employed.

What do we mean by consensus? Likert and Likert suggest it is a willingness to accept the group's conclusions. They say,

> The process of arriving at consensus is a free and open exchange of ideas which continues until agreement has been reached. This process assures that each individual's concerns are heard and understood and that a sincere attempt has been made to take them into consideration in the search for and the formulation of a conclusion. This conclusion may not reflect the exact wishes of each member, but since it does not violate the deep concerns of anyone, it can be agreed upon by all.
>
> Consensus, then, is a cooperative effort to find a solution acceptable to everyone rather than a competitive struggle in which an unacceptable

solution is forced on the losers. With consensus as the pattern of interaction, members need not fear being outsmarted or outmaneuvered. They can be frank, candid, and authentic in their interactions at all steps in the decision-making process.[14]

Two factors interact when a church agrees to support a given alternative before it. The quality of the alternative as it relates to the mission of the church is one factor. The acceptance of an alternative by the people who make it up is a second one. In using consensus there is a danger that quality may be sacrificed to gain acceptance. Yet, no alternative will ever be implemented in the voluntary organization without acceptance by the group responsible for implementing it. There is a practical reality that many innovative changes in a church were once voted down by the same body.

The goal of growth is paramount in decision making. Consensus allows for growth to take place but with the recognition that it will fall short of the ideal. Church groups often bemoan how little they have accomplished. The half-met goal is an agony for any responsible person. But many churches live a guilt-ridden life because their successes are seldom identified and celebrated. If the people of God are able to celebrate their actual growth, they can be empowered for new growth. If failure to achieve the ideal is dominant, the guilt of loss overcomes celebration causing guilt and debilitation occur. Figure 4-3 illustrates the need for celebration of that which has been accomplished.

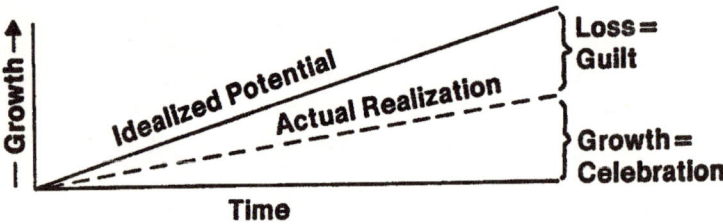

Figure 4-3: Growth for People of God

Second, allow sufficient time for the group to decide. By following consensus processes the decision process cannot be forced to a quick conclusion by a vote. Many decisions which congregations ought to make can be made if given enough time. The effective leader will have enough informal contact with the congregation to know how people will vote before the votes are counted. This is a way to achieve consensus using voting rules. Informal polls are constantly taken within the group until there is agreement and a vote taken. Consensus rules formalize that press.

How much time should a decision take? It depends. The closer together in attractiveness the alternatives and the more varied the information about them, the higher the level of confidence required by a group. The more a decision requires a reversal of previous thought and behavior, the higher the level of confidence required. The more vague the possible outcome of a decision, the higher the confidence level. The higher the level of confidence required, the more time a decision will take. It is far wiser to delay a decision until agreement can be secured than to force a decision which polarizes a congregation into factions. The consequence of such factions is that no action proceeds from a decision, even when it is made.

Stage 3

After the Decision

Reduce Static

by

Reassurance to the Unsure

Support to Losers

Acceptance of a Loss

Humility in Winning

Figure 4-4: Conclusion of Decision Making

Some conflict is generated by decisions. To assume that agreement on an issue ends the debate is an error. To the degree consensus actually exists, it is to that degree a decision resolves conflict.

There is a result of most decisions which we choose to call dissonance or static. It is the feeling of uncertainty, disharmony, or anxiety which follows most decisions. It is possible to feel anxious about an action you have taken even when you believe it is a wise one.

The ministry of reducing static following a decision is an important aspect of promoting sound church relationships. After every decision, one should assume that the task of ministry continues. How can static be reduced?

First, reassure those who are most unsure about the decision. There is a genuine ministry to support given by the pastor who can say, "John, I appreciate the important questions you raised on our long-range plan and want to assure you of my support as we work together to see they are answered to your satisfaction."

Second, help can be given to assist individuals to give up emotional attachments to unchosen alternatives. An unchosen alternative may have been preferable to some who are willing to support the preferences of the larger group. A group of older women in a small class may vote to give their Sunday School space to a larger youth group and feel anger and grief in their decision. If the minister can allow persons to unload their emotional stress in making difficult decisions, the unchosen option can be given up more easily.

Third, it is necessary on occasion to reduce static by learning how to lose. If it is obvious the group supports a direction that is not your own, an agreement to disagree in love may be required. This is especially true for pastoral leaders. There is a dynamic at work in group processes we call "testing the leader." At an early stage of group life it will resist or oppose the leader as a test. If the leader responds openly with minimal threat, growth toward a deeper level of trust and closeness will occur. If the leader asserts authority or resists with anger and attacks, the stage is set for a contest later in the group life. Our conversations with ministry leaders indicate the first such skirmish occurs as the conclusion of the "honeymoon" period of a pastorate. This is three to six months after beginning a new ministry. A second encounter often occurs eighteen to twenty months into the pastorate, which determines the tenure of the ministry. If intimacy grows after this encounter, the tests lengthen to cycles of five-year periods. If the minister sets up a win-lose reaction during these tests, he or she usually relocates into another congregation within a few months.

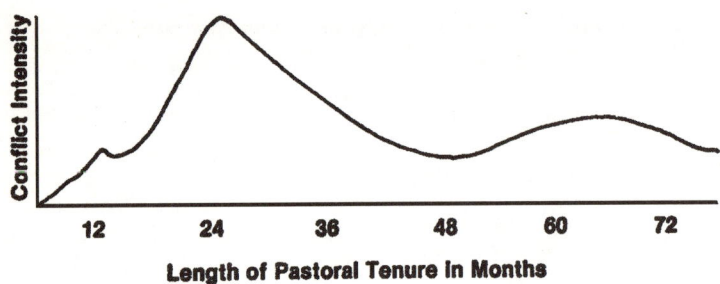

Figure 4-5: Cycles of Conflict Ministry

Finally, reduction of static occurs when there is a victory in a decision. If the decision is interpreted as a group victory by those who led in the process, dissonance lowers. If, however, the leaders gloat in their personal accomplishments, others who were supportive, but anxious, will become resistant to their own decisions. Leaders need to learn how to be good winners.

When things fall apart—In spite of the best intentions and the deepest of spiritual commitments, some churches find themselves in dysfunctional conflict. Every process is dependent upon persons who are fallible. Too often it seems Murphy's well-known law is fixed in the nature of things: "If anything can go wrong, it will!"

No doubt you can recall multiple events in the church when everything went wrong. Permanent estrangement between persons, deeply hurt feelings, members who leave the church, and the church schism are results of the worst forms of conflict. But such events do occur.

A respected leader in the church becomes involved in unethical moral behavior which becomes public knowledge. The congregation quickly "chooses up sides" with one group demanding judgment, another forgiveness. Polarization occurs. Feelings fly high and the full energies of the congregation focus upon this one event for weeks. Ministry and tasks which need so desperately to be done go undone. Conversation after conversation is required for the group to talk through its feelings. At any point in that process factions can become rigid and decisive. Mature wisdom and patience in unusual quantities are demanded of the leadership in such a time.

A personality conflict between the pastor and the most influential lay leader in the church develops. The lay leader is a prominent businessman of the community, from whom many of the church members have bought goods for years. The pastor is relatively young and new in the community. He has identified with a group of newer, young families in the church and has attempted to change the power of the "old guard" in the church. He is thwarted at every move, but continues to push for change. Finally, the entrenched leadership requests his resignation. He refuses. The congregation votes on whether to dismiss him as pastor. The majority votes yes. But the younger members are solidly behind him. Angry charges are hurled from each side after the vote. The pastor announces he is forming a new church and all who will join him should follow him as he leaves the meeting.

These are mild examples of the degree to which conflict can become intense. Physical fighting, abusive telephone calling, even violence, can occur in the name of a religious stance.

While few people desire to be caught up in such emotion-laden conflict, it happens. Are there specific steps that can be taken in the face of traumatic, emotional conflict?

When conflict becomes uncontrollable, it is necessary to resort to rules. When emotions take control, it is important that there be an established process of resolution which at least one party in the conflict insists be followed. Few groups, except mobs, will allow their hostility to grow to such an extent that all rules are suspended. Bylaws, constitutions, minutes of previous meetings, or written agreements can be appealed to as rule documents to ensure some possibility of process.

Second, there must be an individual with skill and control who is not a direct party to the conflict who is responsible for enforcing the rules and guiding the conflict process. Dysfunctional conflict calls for outside intervention. In organizational settings an official outside the congregation may be called upon to serve as a referee and to moderate the discussion as an objective outsider. We are aware of one congregational conflict in which each side requested legal counsel to be present to ensure an abiding by established rules.

It is important, thirdly, to diffuse the conflict as much as possible when it is apparent that its intensity is great. Diffusion can be accomplished by the referral of the conflict to committees, by requesting fact-finding panels from outside the congregation, and by agreeing upon a cooling off period. Time is one of the most important factors in conflict. Postponing discussion and decision on an issue can be a way of dissipating some of the emotional energy attached to it.

Finally, depersonalize the conflict. The issues at hand must be highlighted rather than the specific individuals involved. In a voluntary organization like the church, maximum focus upon personal interaction can occur best by separating issues from the persons involved and dealing with them in this fashion.

Much of the illustrative material in this chapter has dealt with poorly-managed situations. Are guidelines offered here ever practiced in real life? The following case illustrates how one pastor tried to practice a style of leadership which gave precedence to the persons involved rather than the issue involved. Whether or not you agree with his position on neo-Pentecostalism, how do you feel about his work in this situation? Which of the guidelines offered here are apparent in the case? Which was he successful in using, and which ineffective? We have imposed the stages of our process in the margins of the case to illustrate the process does work!

STEP 1
Spotting
Conflict
Potential

a. **Interpersonal Stress**

Conflict over carrying out the church ministry surfaced with a group of neo-Pentecostals in the church two years ago. Beginning with a couple of families, the group steadily grew for over a year without its strength being realized. I first became aware of the movement when one of our members informed me that her Sunday School teacher suggested she get a divorce when an unsuccessful exorcism attempt provoked considerable conflict between her and her supposedly "demon-possessed" husband. I discovered

b. Dissatisfaction

STEP 2
Avoidance
with Integrity

a. Gather Facts
b. Open
   Communication

STEP 3
Engagement
by Diffusion

a. Personal
   Initiative
b. Public Acknowl-
   edgment

that five of our teachers were neo-Pentecostals who had replaced our denominational literature with their own. Also, four of these women's husbands had key leadership positions and were highly critical of the church's program. My greatest concern at this point was determining how many people were involved and what effect their teaching was having on individuals and church life. My hope was ultimately to bring into light what heretofore had been highly secretive; to do it in such a way as not to castigate anyone; and if possible, to handle the situation so as to make room for differences of faith, keeping all parties in the church.

The following background information gives you some perspective about my situation. Unknown to the pulpit committee at the time of my call, and still unrealized a year later by most members, the neo-Pentecostal group had been quietly at work within the church, making converts. The group singled out individuals with emotional, psychological, or physical problems. These people were invited to a charismatic's home, supposedly for a social affair. However, following a brief period of refreshments, newcomers were ushered into the customary discussion/prayer meeting which was accompanied by speaking in tongues, laying on of hands, casting out demons, and healing. Also, the tongues group seized upon a desire of adult members to discuss more relevant issues as an opportunity to inject their own materials. After a good number had been exposed to these "social evenings" and classes, conflict emerged over the covert manner, superior attitude, and divisiveness of the charismatics. Some members became distraught; others were intimidated when their salvation was questioned. By this time, members began to approach me. A doctor whose wife was involved, claimed their differing religious views threatened their marriage. The situation began to polarize charismatics and resisting church members.

I first attempted to assess the movement's strength and extent. In talking with members of the group, I explained to them the necessity for openness concerning their experiences due to the disturbance and confusion in the church. I chose the following Sunday morning to acknowledge the situation from the pulpit. Realizing emotions were too high to give biblical interpretation to the pros and cons of tongues speaking, I explicitly stated

c. Neutrality

d. Availability

e. Delay

STEP 4
Conclusion

that I was *not* preaching a sermon; rather, I expressed a low-keyed concern for the interests of both neo-Pentecostals and others, that we respect varying experiences without making anyone's experience normative for all Christians. Following the service, I avoided taking my usual position at the door lest the comments of some might offend or challenge others nearby. Now that the situation was out in the open, considerable tension was alleviated. During the following weeks, I counseled with two couples whose marriages had been in upheaval, visited disturbed members, and met with the most aggressive leaders of the neo-Pentecostals. The most outspoken couples interpreted my low-keyed talk as a sign the Holy Spirit was "dealing with" me. During the three times we met, they inevitably proposed to lay hands on me to confer an experience like theirs. I shared my Christian experience with them, but they would not accept it as valid. Several months later, this couple formed a charismatic church in their home. Eight other couples joined them. After this departure, I used our midweek service to discuss the neo-Pentecostal movement and to give biblical interpretation of key Scriptures associated with it.

My ultimate goal of retaining divergent groups within the fellowship was largely not successful. I felt my hands were tied in trying to mediate, partly because of the advanced state of the conflict before I became aware of it. Study sessions following the charismatic withdrawal may have been helpful in preventing others from being led away. On the positive side, the conflict gave greater incentive for serious Bible study and greater concern for people's needs. I feel I was primarily effective in maintaining an open, honest relationship with the neo-Pentecostals which lasts to this day. Since the conflict, three couples have come by to express how much the church had meant to them. Two couples returned to the church. Three other couples wrote asking that their names be removed from our rolls, and expressed their love and prayerful concern for the church.

The quality of ministry with organizational conflict is dependent upon many factors—leadership, core commitment of the congregation, the issues which confront it, and its organizational structures. Serious attention to those controllable factors of leadership, structures, and core values are first steps in creating the kind of community which demonstrates its Christian faith by the way it ministers to persons in the midst of its own conflict.

Community Conflict: When Controversy Comes to Our City

The need for conflict ministry may arise from external as well as internal sources. So far in this book we have emphasized the personal and internal sources of conflict with which churches must deal. Community change, community issues, or controversies which spill into a congregation from its larger environment also provide challenge for conflict ministry. The consequence of this is that many congregational leaders strive to insulate the church from any such influences. The attitude often emerges, "That is really none of the church's business," in the face of controversial issues. Such an attitude keeps church members from understanding the full meaning of the Christian gospel as it impacts daily life.

Church and community in interaction—An understanding of the church engaged in conflict ministry in the community rests upon a conception of the interaction between church and community. Their relation is one of reciprocity. Each acts upon and is acted upon by the other. Change which occurs within religious institutions will have long term effects upon the larger systems of the social order.[15] Change within social systems will have immediate impact upon religious institutions.[16]

Since we have suggested earlier that personal conflict is rooted in the stresses created by change, it is appropriate to view changes in systems as a stress upon the parts of that system. Every community is a social system of interactive parts. Those parts are subsystems of the larger whole. These subsystems of a community consist of economics, government, education, communication, public health, law enforcement, religion, cultural arts, and recreation. Each of these exist in institutional forms in order to meet basic human needs for existence, security, belonging, and contributing. When rapid change, disequilibrium, or conflict occurs in any of the institutions of a community, human needs are often neglected. The crises precipitated by such unmet human needs affect the functioning of persons who, in turn, make up the systems of the community. Among the first subsystems to experience the jolts of change are the "soft" institutions—those people-oriented structures which exist to provide support and care for individuals. These include families, social welfare agencies, churches, and other voluntary community agencies. Perhaps we can illustrate this from recent events in our community.

We live in a community which has lived through the conflict generated by court-ordered busing as a means of desegregating the educational system. Because of resistance by educational leaders to the inevitable, the busing order was mandated only two weeks prior to the opening of school in 1975. Major changes had to be made quickly to comply with the order. Too few buses were available, requiring split shifts for school classes. Suddenly, families were caught up in the stresses of getting children ready for school from 6:00 AM to

8:30 AM. Car pool schedules had to be changed. New schools in distant parts of the city were assigned to certain pupils. Some feared the move to schools in neighborhoods where the pupils would be a minority race. Anger erupted. Sunday School classes became centers for the discussion of only one topic—busing. Racial hostility oozed from the lips of formerly placid church members. Cursing, then marches, bombs, and violence marked the opening of school. Boycotts were announced against stores and businesses which would not openly advertise antibusing sentiments. Those who did so felt opposite pressures from pro-busing customers. White church members stalked out of worship services in which a reconciling word was proclaimed. Courageous leaders emerged to call for calm only to receive intimidating phone calls. Conflict swept the whole community and there was no neutral ground. You were either "pro" or "con" on busing.

In the early days of the controversy, reaction ruled the day. But in the calmer reflections of the days following the initial shock of change, proactive groups began to emerge to deal with the change. Discussion groups sprang up in churches and schools. Visits by parents to distant schools were scheduled. Major business groups like the Chamber of Commerce began studies to focus upon school system improvements. Media groups adopted news policies designed to prevent exaggeration of minor incidents in the schools. Ecumenical groups attacked the issue through task forces promoting calm and open communication. Now, several years later, sanity prevails, constructive improvements are occurring within the schools, and more racial balance exists. Yet public-school education has lost much of its support in the process of all these feelings of conflict. The slightest controversy over a school matter reopens festering sores of anger and hostility.

Does this mean that churches can only *react* to conflict in the community? No, but reaction is one of the inevitable results of community conflict. Those churches which are able to take decisive action in the face of controversy are prepared for it. They have studied issues and their responses to them before the conflict and have developed lay support for action.

Any system change requires a model for change which is supported by the elements of the system which is changed. Models are conceptual devices for explaining reality.[17] The model for the church we propose is one which defines the church as an intentional voluntary community led by one who understands and organizes change. What are the elements of this model?

First, as a voluntary organization, any church's members are free not to participate in its life and work. Unfortunately, this often means that laity can easily withdraw their participation, financial support, or membership in the face of controversy. No congregation can be any stronger in dealing with conflict than the commitment of its members to struggle with the integrity of church membership.

Most congregations are formed on the basis of sociological factors which are more rooted in the income, educational, and occupational factors of social class, race, family background, and social mobility aspirations than theological factors, per se.

Therefore, how a given congregation deals with controversy rests upon the perceptions of the social group it attracts. The more a group sees its commitment to following Jesus Christ as contrasting with the social or cultural expectations of its community, the more difficult conflict will be for it. Such a group is intensely supportive of each person within it. The members try to love each other and serve each other as a source of strength for being different from their neighbors. Conflict can shatter easily such a group.

Second, the work of a congregation is a collaborative process between clergy and laity. Communication between both is essential if a group of church members is to develop its capacities to become involved in external issues. In American churches clergy tend to be more committed to involvement of the church in controversial issues than laity.[18] Thus, this difference of perception may become a critical stress point for the activist leader.

The first step in the collaborative process needs to be a verbal declaration of intentions and feelings by both clergy and laity about church involvement in the community. Second, Bible studies, discussion groups on current issues, and special seminars are essential dialogical tools for a congregation to develop its perspective on ministry.

Not only must educational strategies be employed to lead persons to identify and talk about their differences, congregations must help persons struggle with their differences within a supportive context in order to facilitate specific actions. Action begins in study. But study which leads to no consequences becomes sterile. However feeble the attempt, churches learn by doing. So the goal of collaboration is to help groups identify their gifts in responding to community concerns and *actually becoming involved in doing something about them.*

Donald W. Shriver, Jr., and Karl A. Ostrom recently studied a group of residents in the North Carolina urban triangle of cities—Raleigh, Durham, and Chapel Hill. Their concern was to find persons who scored high on four marks of ethical maturity. These were "action potential" or a disposition to act on personal beliefs, "public regard," or a willingness to sacrifice private interests for the common good, "racial openness," or interest in all persons, and "trust" or affirmation of life with emotional wholeness.[19] They summarized:

> The chances that any persons will score *high* on any mark *increases* with

(1) increasing political involvement, (2) increasing participation in a church that affirms public religion, and (3) increasingly satisfying relations with one's friends. In short, the core ethical dispositions of the Judeo-Christian tradition are best nourished when (1) political activity in public life, (2) worship in a religious community, and (3) interpersonal dialogue on the meaning of faith for all of life are *found together in the lives of people.*[20]

A third aspect of negotiating intentional ministry concerns the needs of clergy to find personal and professional support for a change oriented leadership. In the process of collaboration between clergy and laity a certain tension is inevitable. Intentional ministry requires support for clergy both within and outside the church. We are convinced, based upon extensive conversations with clergy persons, that loneliness is the most pronounced feeling of the change-oriented minister.[21] The clergy is the only professional group in our society dependent upon the group it serves for both the level of its income and its supervision. Reward systems are determined almost wholly by others—either within the congregation or the denominational hierarchy. The latter is usually based upon a perception of the former. Given this reality, the temptation of the minister is often to capitulate to the lowest common denominator of expectations within the congregation or lash out in anger against those who are served. Rather than do either, pastoral leaders can seek friendships and support.

The fourth aspect of our model involves the negotiation of intent. Congregations must negotiate their way toward community involvement. Clergy must utilize the processes of negotiation if churches are to grow in their degree of commitment to community involvement. John E. Biersdorf has provided a helpful understanding of negotiation as referring to the "quality of relationships and the transactions by which ministry is carried out."[22] Negotiation begins as an intentional act by the leader of self-consciously choosing his/her role identity, faith stance, and expectations of consequences.

The leader then builds a constituency around that constellation of intentionality. The negotiation model requires three things of the congregational leader:[23]
- Assist the congregation to dream a dream of what it can be and do with its community. Changing life requires a vision of that which is beyond the present reality. Jesus was teaching his disciples to pray for dreams in his modeling phrase, "Thy kingdom come,/Thy will be done, On earth as it is in heaven" (Matt. 6:10).
- Build a community of people around that dream by working for consensus in sharing the dream. Community action is collective action. Help must be given to others for understanding issues and for

CONGREGATIONAL FIGHTS

understanding the tensions which come from addressing them.
- The multiple, individual gifts of the group must be integrated into a wholistic response to the issues at hand. Not every person can make the same contribution, but each can make some contribution. Effective leadership motivates others to give out of their uniqueness to the common tasks of fulfilling the congregation's dream.

These are the elements of our model—a voluntary association of people interacting with the community led by intentional persons building a constituency around a dream. How well a given congregation may be able to become intentional depends upon its commitment and setting.

Types of congregations and community issues—How a congregation responds to conflict in the community arena rests on its nature as a social reality. Many idealists expect the same ability for action from every group. This ignores the fundamental requirement that a group have resources beyond survival if it is to be proactive in its ministry. Some congregations, by virtue of their size, income, location, and organization, can be more directly involved in controversy than others. Can we classify congregations in terms of their possibilities for community action?

The *communal group* is often formed as a proactive response to a particular issue. Its small size, tightly-woven fellowship, and explicit expectations give it the capacity to face specific issues with abandon. Communal forms of church life have influence in effecting change far beyond their apparent resources. Who can measure the awareness created on specific issues by groups such as Koinonia Farms in South Georgia,[24] the Christian World Liberation Front in Berkeley, California,[25] or Emmaus House in New York City?[26] Because consensus decision making is at the heart of communal group life a focused response can be made by such groups. The group of 30 fully committed people can influence change far out of proportion to its size.

Such groups, however, tend to be limited to singular issues. Small groups have energy and financial resources for restricted involvements. They must limit themselves to a concentrated engagement with one issue. Highly complex issues or controversies which extend beyond the local community become so draining that many small intentional communities "burn out" with time.[27] Networking among groups and coalition-building are useful strategies for the linking of resources. But often such strategies require such investments of time that one begins to feel that the group is part of an incredibly institutional approach to change. Most communal groups resist such an expenditure of effort in building an organization.

Another form of congregation is the *sect* church. This small, emotional, and informal church form chooses strategies of noninvolvement in community conflict. By definition, sects tend to be withdrawn from the community arena of action. Sect groups are most successful, ironically, among the community groups who suffer most acutely when unjust community decisions are made. Minority, racial, ethic, and poverty groups identify most with sectarian forms of church life. Thus, the very people who most need a church involved in the community find their religious needs met by forms of faith which give hope primarily of a meaningful future community.

This dilemma poses a challenge for mainline denominations in their development of strategies for communities of the dispossessed and alienated. Sectarian forms such as storefront churches, lay-led mission groups, and small, family churches or emotional religion can be linked with social ministry and social action forms of ministry. Such groups can be approached by mainline groups as meaningful participants in diagnosing community needs and issues. With acceptance of different ministry forms, such groups may be encouraged to become involved in concerns which will result in significant community change.

The predominant type of church is the *neighborhood church.* It is in the neighborhood church that one finds the most interaction between church and community. As a subunit of the neighborhood the church is a major element of its identity and function. Churches can be more powerful in influencing community change at this level than at any other. It is also at this level that neighborhood change most affects congregations, whether positively or negatively. "As goes the neighborhood, so goes the church" has often been the attitude of congregational leaders. It is also often true that "As goes the church, so goes the neighborhood." Most issues or changes which come to a neighborhood will eventually influence the churches within it.

Because of this fact, many churches in recent years have bonded together to act positively as a force for strengthening the neighborhood in which they are located. Cluster ministries have emerged all across the United States to fulfill such a function.

One such ministry is the Highlands Community Ministry Incorporated, in Louisville, Kentucky. It formed in the mid-1960s as a nonprofit corporation supported by Protestant churches of several denominations. It began with a coordinated program of ministries serving the people of the community— after-school care for children, preschool nursery care, recreation programs, and a program for singles. In time Roman Catholic Churches joined in the effort as the work expanded to provide a day care for elderly persons, and a wide diversity of neighborhood ministries. Attention has been focused upon housing problems and a strong voice in the neighborhood is present to communicate needs to governmental and social agencies. Because of this, the neighborhood continues to be a vital residential community in which people of many types choose to live. This allows churches to have a continuing ministry

CONGREGATIONAL FIGHTS

where other similar neighborhoods have deteriorated, lost population, and watched their churches disband.

A major factor in church responsiveness to neighborhood change is time. If congregations do not monitor slow change, its impact may come into consciousness too late to have an influence upon it. Rapid change may trigger such negative reactions that the congregation polarizes in conflict and declines. The latter fate was the experience of a congregation we shall call Parkview Church.

Located in an urban neighborhood of a large metropolis, this church appeared to have a bright future in 1969. It saw itself as a growing suburban congregation with plans to expand its facilities. According to the 1970 census the church was located in a predominantly white, middle-class neighborhood. During 1970, two new public housing facilities of 335 multifamily units were opened for occupancy. In 1972 an additional 100 units were constructed. More than 90 percent of the new residents in the community were black and poor. Immediately the racial and economic character of the school system changed. Massive white flight occurred. Within three years the school nearest the church changed from 542 white students to 426 black students and 165 white students. Rumors of racial conflict spread through the area, each being followed by "For Sale" signs. Businesses began to relocate or close. Boy Scout and Girl Scout troops could find no leaders for a period of time. Three nearby churches disbanded and sold their properties to black congregations. Other churches remaining in the community declined from 50 to 80 percent in attendance. Parkview Church declined from a weekly average Sunday School attendance in 1969 of 255 to 103 in 1974.

In spite of its tradition of being located in a historically segregated city, the church's policy and attitude were racially inclusive. Yet it was unable to make a transition in responding to its new neighborhood constituency at the pace in which it changed racially and economically. Both the pastor and congregation found themselves grieved, depressed, and debilitated by the conflicts they had experienced.

A fourth style of church is the *regional church*. This congregation serves a geographic area larger than a neighborhood but only a sector of the metropolitan community. Its constituency tends to be relatively homogeneous as the congregation attracts persons on the basis of social factors rather than geographic ones. If the regional church is to be involved in its community, it will more likely respond to those issues which confront the larger community. It is relatively well insulated from the local concerns of individual neighborhoods. Because it is nongeographical in identity its future is seldom linked to the fate of one neighborhood area within its sector of ministry.

Community issues of justice and equality do confront such churches. The tensions of labor-management disputes within local employment, political decision making, race relations, educational concerns, women's liberation, homosexuality, medical ethics, and national policy questions are ever-present realities.

The final style of congregation we will consider is "Old First Church." Located in the central core of a metropolis it is usually the most diverse of the congregational types. Because of its central city location it must appeal to rich and poor, black and white, and young and old if it is to survive. Both its diversity and location provide opportunities for a metropolitan-wide concern in its multiple ministries.[28]

Old First church must have the stance of both a neighborhood church and a regional church. A significant part of its ministry is bound up in the neighborhood in which it is located. Critical income, housing, and health needs are paramount for its central city residents. Yet, its ability to maintain viable neighborhood ministries rests upon its successes in attracting suburban commuter families for worship and service. So this congregation must interact with both neighborhood and metropolitan issues in its conflict ministry.

Ministry amid conflict and change—The thrust of this book has been upon a proactive involvement in conflict ministry. Nowhere is this emphasis more apparent as a need than in the community arena. For the congregation to assume a reactive stance within its community makes it a pawn in the ever-shifting moods and currents of the larger environment. Churches must equip their members for active involvement in the community arena. But how?

First, churches can minister with the victims of conflict within community social structures. A critical conflict ministry is a crisis ministry of making help available for modern Samaritans who travel the trafficways of the modern metropolis (Luke 10:25-37). Every church can invest its prayer, energies, money, and volunteers in developing better care for the victims of a world in conflict. The poor, imprisoned, ill, infirm, alcoholic, hungry, and unemployed within any community cry out for support and help. Congregational, ecumenical, and denominational programs of providing professional assistance to meet human need at the survival level will always be a major agenda for the ministering church. Neither must one overlook the spiritual ministry of sharing the gospel of hope. There is a balm of Gilead for the victims of our social systems which is the good news of Jesus Christ. Let us not fail to share that in the caring support that churches can and should give to the victim.

The second agenda of the church for conflict ministry is education. Shriver and Ostrom have called for the realization of two fantasies they have about churches in mission. They are the development of both Sunday School and preaching as teaching the application of Scripture to modern life.[29] Persons are not prepared to act in the community forum for faith until they are aware of the issues. We are convinced that the reason more Christians are not involved in meaningful ministry outside the church is that too little of the discussion, debate, and dialogue of church education is directed outside itself. Churches can be the universities of learning about community problems, their effects upon persons, and the complexity of meaningful solutions to them.

Third, the congregation should become a personal support structure empowering individuals in the fulfillment of their calling in the world. Much of the best ministry of the church is the action of persons with a Christian conscience who are involved responsibly within their vocations, as volunteers in ministry programs, through participation in political decisions, and by means of involvement on community boards and agencies. Yet, every person's energies are limited. The church must be a place where those kinds of investments are recognized, encouraged and supported. Every activist needs a group with whom frustrations and disappointments can be shared and victories celebrated.

Fourth, churches can be prophetic voices condemning social wrong and calling for just systems. There are conditions of injustice within the community which need the address of collective church opposition. At this level of action individual congregation involvement is most effective through participation in denominational and ecumenical groups who have greater power than one group. Systems contain power within themselves of such strength that collective church action is required if change is to occur in this arena.

The nature of conflict itself is another reason for collective action by church groups. Given the voluntary nature of the congregation we have described, few congregations can secure sufficient consensus to act with enough force to confront effectively community injustice. Larger groupings, however, provide greater resources for employing social action specialists or community organizers for greater expertise. They also provide a buffer for the congregation to support meaningful change with less threat to its existence. Collective witness through resolutions, press releases, media presentations, drama, art, and publications have their impact in declaring Christian concern about specific social problems.

There are dangers in such forms of action, however. Whenever such involvement replaces the primary work of the church in evangelizing and growing persons in Christian discipleship, it should be avoided. Neither should churches use their power to impose a particular political position upon others nor baptize a partisan candidate or issue in the name of Christ. The principle of separation of church and state is a cherished principle in American democratic society. This means the government should not have the power to control or enforce religious beliefs. It also means the church must not control nor dictate its wishes to the state. Efforts to develop so-called "Christian parties" will dilute the gospel of Jesus Christ into the use of the church to support the aims of sinful persons.

Churches also must be engaged, as a fifth strategy for involvement, in organized action. Congregations can support individuals within them, denominational agencies, ecumenical networks, and coalitions of religious and secular groups in specific forms of action. While no persons should be forced to participate in any way which violates individual conscience, each should be free to act as he or she chooses in community issues. Some will choose to volunteer to work in a Christian social ministry agency, others to seek elective political office, or participation in community issues. Some will feel private conversation with community leaders, letter writing, or prayer for decision makers best suits their dispositions and beliefs. What must be recognized is that each can be a legitimate form of involvement. Congregations could do well to mobilize every member to participate in at least one of these actions on a specific issue or need. It would change the character of the communities in which we live.

The witness of silence—Many readers of this chapter will react negatively to the suggestions which have been made in it; for there is a very strong feeling among a large number of contemporary Christians that the best witness for the church in the face of conflict is silence. It is argued, in support of this feeling, that faith is personal and private. For the church to confront community realities is to step beyond the bounds of the private and offend those who hold a contrary view.

Such is the risk every activist group must take. Yet there is a more fundamental concern which activist faith must raise and that is the corporate consequences which result from silence itself.

We would suggest that congregational silence about a church's community is itself a form of community action. A church which withdraws from the arena of conflict gives support to the winner. Silence in the face of economic struggles between rich and poor is a form of action in support of the winners of that struggle—the rich. The response of silence to the discrimination of minorities is a support for the majority. Silence in the face of violence, sexual exploitation of women and children, hunger, and inadequate shelter simply reinforces whoever wins in the struggle between the powers of darkness and light.

The ultimate question which one must raise concerns the nature of the gospel itself. In the ministry of Jesus and the record of the gospel does one find silence as a workable strategy for confronting conflict? Actually, the opposite finding is the case. The words of peace, forgiveness, wholeness, repentance, judgment, and grace were pronounced by word and deed upon the structures of this present world. Let us follow the example of Jesus and become active *peacemakers* in a world of conflict. Not every conflict was laid to rest when he spoke. Anger and hostility were the reaction of those who were judged by his words and

CONGREGATIONAL FIGHTS 115

deeds. Silence may be more comfortable in the face of injustice and wrong. But if they win, there will be no comfort. When God's rule and reign become complete, justice and righteousness will be established eternally. It is the hope of that promise which gives the church boldness to act as a minister amid conflict in the community.

Notes:
[1] James D. Anderson and Ezra Earl Jones, *The Management of Ministry* (New York: Harper and Row, 1978), pp. 17-25.
[2] Dean M. Kelley, *Why Conservative Churches Are Growing* (New York: Harper and Row, 1971).
[3] Dean R. Hoge, *Division in the Protestant House* (Philadelphia: The Westminster Press, 1976), pp. 66-69.
[4] John S. Savage, *The Apathetic and Bored Church Member* (Pittsford, NY: LEAD Consultants, 1976) pp. 62-71, 91-98.
[5] Alan C. Filley, *Interpersonal Conflict Resolution* (Glenview, Illinois: Scott, Foresman and Co., 1974), pp. 4-5.
[6] Edward B. Lindaman, *Thinking in the Future Tense* (Nashville: Broadman Press, 1978), p. 83.
[7] Savage, pp. 45-47.
[8] *Ibid.*, pp. 68-71.
[9] Anderson and Jones, pp. 49-50.
[10] Filley, p. 25.
[11] Rensis and Jane Gibson Likert, *New Ways of Managing Conflict* (New York: McGraw-Hill Book Co., 1976), p. 141.
[12] See E. Warren Rust, Comp., *The Mobile American and Multifamily Housing* (Atlanta: Home Mission Board, S.B.C., 1976) for an analysis of the implications of mobility for ministry.
[13] See Likert and Likert, pp. 157-181.
[14] Likert and Likert, p. 146.
[15] Space does not permit a full discussion of the extensive literature in the sociology of religion which reinforces this assertion. Weberian social theory emphasizes this dimension of the social impact of religious change. See J. Alan Winter, *Continuities of the Sociology of Religion* (New York: Harper and Row, 1977), pp. 54-78 for recent Weberian research.
[16] Those who emphasize this dimension of change tend to follow Durkheimian's social theory. See Robert Bellah, "Religious Evolution," *Beyond Belief* (New York: Harper and Row, 1970), pp. 20-50 for an excellent brief discussion of the impact of social change upon religion throughout history.
[17] Paul Meadows, "Models, Systems and Science," *American Sociological Review* 22:3-9, February, 1957.
[18] Jeffrey Hadden has documented the differences between clergy and laity on theological and civil rights issues in *The Gathering Storm in the Churches* (Garden City, NY: Doubleday & Co., Inc., 1970). More specific data on clergy beliefs and involvement in social issues may be found in Harold E. Quinley, *The Prophetic Clergy: Social Activism Among Protestant Ministers* (New York: John Wiley & Sons, 1974), esp. pp. 49-72, 185-209.
[19] Donald W. Shriver, Jr., and Karl A. Ostrom, *Is There Hope for the City?* (Philadelphia: The Westminster Press, 1977), pp. 103-113.
[20] *Ibid.*, p. 109.
[21] Henri Nouwen's poignant reflections confirm the assertion. See *The Wounded Healer* (Garden City, NY: Doubleday & Co., Inc., 1972), pp. 81-100.
[22] John E. Biersdorf (ed.), *Creating an Intentional Ministry* (Nashville: Abingdon Press, 1976), p. 13.
[23] Adapted from *Creating an Intentional Ministry*, p. 18.
[24] Dallas Lee, *The Cotton Patch Evidence* (New York: Harper and Row, 1971).
[25] Donald Heinz, "The Christian World Liberation Front," *The New Religious Consciousness*

ed. by Charles Y. Glock and Robert N. Bellah (Berkeley: University of California Press, 1976), pp. 143-161.

[26] John E. Biersdorf, *Hunger For Experience: Vital Religious Communities in America Today* (New York: The Seabury Press, 1975), p. 146. Other communal and intentional communities are described and studied in this book.

[27] Jeffrey K. Hadden and Charles F. Longino, Jr., *Gideon's Gang* (Philadelphia: Pilgrim Press, 1974) is a case study documenting the difficulties of sustaining a congregation founded as an intentional social action group.

[28] Ezra Earl Jones and Robert L. Wilson, *What's Ahead for Old First Church* (New York: Harper and Row, 1974).

[29] Shriver and Ostrom, pp. 162-165.

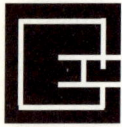

The Continuing Education Unit •

Assignment

1. While conflict is a "neutral word" it has consequences. Identify and briefly describe both the positive and negative consequences of organizational conflict.

2. Outline a plan of action to turn a "win-lose" situation into a "win-win" situation.

3. Define "consensus." Give reasons why this method of decision-making has value.

4. What is the single most important key to depersonalizing conflict?

5. Review the case study on neo-Pentecostalism. Answer the questions on page 102.

6. Explain the following phrases relating to community conflict:
   (a) "collaborative process."
   (b) "negotiation of intent."

7. Differentiate the following congregational forms:
   (a) the "communal group."
   (b) the "sect church."
   (c) the "neighborhood church."
   (d) the "regional church."
   (e) the "Old First Church."

8. Confronted with the reality of conflict in a community, should a congregation be "proactive" or exercise "silence"? Defend your answer.

Chapter 5

Styles and Resources for Conflict Ministry

How do you tend to react when faced with a situation of conflict? Some people become flustered, feel their stomach muscles tighten, and want to get away from the engagement as soon as possible. For others, conflict is a challenge, like a new game to be mastered. They are poised for battle and ready to take on all opponents.

It is not enough to be able to understand and to analyze various dimensions of conflict. Our personalities, previous experience, and training cause us to react in patterned ways to conflict. We call this pattern of reaction a style of conflict ministry. We want to describe various style which people use in conflict so you can determine your own style. We will also describe the advantages and disadvantages of each style for specific kinds of conflict situations.

Types of Conflict Ministers

There are basically five types of conflict ministers. Most people will tend to respond to all conflict similarly, regardless of the nature of the conflict. This natural reaction to every conflict situation is called one's primary style of ministry. People often get nicknames because their approach to life can be so readily seen. This was true of the disciple named Joseph of Cyprus. In the early years of the New Testament church he became such a helpful and respected leader he was given the name Barnabas which means son of encouragement (Acts 4:36-37).

On the other hand, few persons function from the same perspective at all times and in every situation. If one's primary style of conflict ministry does not prove satisfactory, other approaches will be attempted. The fact that Barnabas was an encourager did not mean he was unwilling to stand his ground and show his temper. "Sharp contention" developed between Paul and him over whether to take John Mark with them on the second missionary journey from Antioch. His commitment to be an encourager to Mark required a break in his relationship with Paul (Acts 15:36-41). So most persons are flexible in their styles of ministry; they employ secondary approaches depending upon the circumstances of the conflict.

The problem solver—The first style of conflict minister is the problem solver. This is the individual who works within conflict to bring forth the best possible conclusion for all of the parties engaged in friction. Such a person is unafraid of sharp expressions of opinion and is willing to keep pressing for conversation and negotiation when others would give up.

Paul was a problem solver in the manner in which he executed his collection ministry in the early Gentile churches. Two problems had emerge in the early Christian community to which he wished to address his ministry. One was the poverty of the original community of faith in Jerusalem as a result of food shortages (Acts 11:27-30; Gal. 2:10). The other was intense conflict over the necessity of circumcision as a requirement for Christian faith (Acts 15; Gal. 2:1-10; 5:1-6). Paul conceived of a large collection from all of the churches he had begun throughout Asia Minor as a symbol of God's healing both problems. The money would meet the needs of poor Christians in Jerusalem. But, more importantly, it would communicate to others the validity of his ministry to Gentiles who had not been circumcised. So he wrote a sermon to circulate to the churches calling them to follow Christ's example in giving (2 Cor. 8, 9), developed a theological explanation of the purpose of the collection (Rom. 15:14-29), organized a method for systematic collection (1 Cor. 16:1-4), and steadfastly delivered the gift in the face of opposition and persecution (Acts 19—21). Paul had set forth a worthy goal as a reasonable response to critical problems and refused to allow conflict to rob either Gentiles or Jewish Christians of the blessings of participation in the collection. He encouraged giving without demanding it, suffered hurt at the hands of his opponents, and became God's agent for the sharing of God's salvation for all persons. His collection ministry was truly a ministry of reconciliation at the point of one of the most profound conflicts of Christian history.[1]

The problem-solver style is the preferable style for dealing with conflict.[2] This is an ideal form of approach to which no one can conform in every ministry situation. The problem solver is committed to the concept of conflict as a failure in communicating concerning the possibility of mutually compatible group goals. Thus, it is most effective as a style in those settings in which communication differences characterize the nature of the conflict.

The problem solver is a specialist in group process and decision making. He or she seeks to help all of the participants of the conflict to verbalize conflict in depersonalized ways. A constructive search for the most satisfying conclusions is sought through a process of information gathering, development of alternative courses of action, listing alternatives in order of priority, and choosing the most beneficial priority for all of the parties involved.

The advantage of this approach is that the problem solver does not fear conflict. It is engaged aggressively for that is the healthiest way to minister when it is present amid a group. However, a high level of concern for all persons in the conflict is maintained. In order to achieve such objectives the problem solver works to develop and maintain high levels of trust within the conflict group. As trust is developed, equally high levels of exposure must accompany trust. The problem solver recognizes that exposure cannot precede trust.

The weaknesses of such a style are several. Some conflict situations do not lend themselves to problem solving. Highly explosive emotional issues are often beyond a problem-solving approach. Settings, in which factions of a group select mutually exclusive goals, do not lend themselves to problem solving. Moreover, a certain level of maturity is required within the group for the problem solving process to work. Other styles may be preferable, depending upon these kinds of factors.

The super helper—The second style of conflict minister is the super helper. This is the person who is constantly working to help others with little concern for self. Such an individual is basically passive in conflicts which affect him or her but will be quite involved with assisting others as they work through their conflicts. Aaron was such a minister. He became a helper for a fearful Moses who could not speak the word of God he felt so deeply (Ex. 4:10-17). As the mouthpiece, administrator, and constant companion of Moses, Aaron became the assistant through whom Moses was able to exercise leadership. The gift of Aaron was the gift of support to another with little concern for himself. It is not surprising that the tribe of Aaron became the tribe of priests in Israel. To be a true priest to another is to be one who supports with care, counsel, and compassion.

There is a serious liability for this style of conflict minister. The super helper is so concerned for the care and support of others that he or she may ignore personal needs for self-support. Super helpers believe their calling is to others. As a consequence they often give so much their own physical, mental, family, spiritual, and economic well-being can be threatened. According to the Scriptures love for God and for others should be balanced with love for oneself (Luke 10:25-28). This is not selfish love but love based upon a relationship with God and with those around us.

The super helper loves others intensely. This leader stands ready to be available to people even when rest and time for spiritual renewal are needed. Helpers assist others as they deal with their anger and frustration; their own remain internal and go unreleased. Helpers work with people to give affirmation and support in times of crisis. Yet, they feel guilty when others affirm them. The helper suffers the risk of becoming a "dry well." The problem of "burnout" which increasing numbers of persons experience in helping professions—teaching, social work, counseling, and professional ministry—is the result of too much giving and too little receiving.

This does not mean helpers are not needed. Quite the contrary! Rather, what is needed is encouragement to those who help to set limits on their helping. The problem solver is a helper as effectively as the super helper. The difference is that a problem-solving approach emphasizes the meeting of the needs of all parties in a conflict. The helper and the one helped are helped equally in a problem-solving approach to ministry.

There are unique occasions in which the super helper approach is most effective. When the basis of conflict is primarily emotional, this style of conflict ministry is needed. In most conflicts there are dimensions of emotional, attitudinal, and substantive differences which garble the communication involved. But some conflicts are clearly emotional in nature. There is basically a clash of personalities at the root of problems. Or, individuals with deep-seated emotional dysfunctions are creating chaos in relating to other persons. Or, there is an irrational reaction to an issue with little willingness to seek facts, explore differences, or communicate about what is happening. In such settings, the style of conflict ministry needed is that of the super helper.

The super helper is especially useful for persons facing the intrapersonal conflict of stress. Such persons are good listeners and can often be directive when relating to the needs of others. Likewise, persons encountering interpersonal stress turn to super helpers.

The power broker—The third style of conflict minister is the power broker. This is the individual who uses the power available to achieve his or her goals in a specific situation. The power broker is committed to win a position, an issue, an argument, or a dream. It is a risky style, for this persons must use every resource to achieve the goal. There are only winners and losers in the power game.

No more vivid example of this is available in the Bible than Elijah's contest with the priests of Baal. He challenged them because Ahab, the king of Israel, had led the nation toward the worship of Baal. His dramatic confrontation was made out of the conviction the God of Israel's heritage would vindicate Himself before His people. Elijah prevailed as fire consumed the offering he had prepared, while the priests of Baal could muster no power. As an evidence of total victory, Elijah had them killed.

There are some situations in which the exercise of power is a necessary act for concluding conflict. Some conflicts are so rooted in substantive feelings or ideas that mutually inclusive goals are not possible. Where the differences in the conflict are substantively contradictory, power must be employed to settle the differences.

As an example, a church cannot be both racially inclusive and racially exclusive in its membership policies. Either all are welcome or they are not. If rigidly entrenched factions are divided on the issue, someone must apply power to conclude it. There will be winners and losers whenever the application of power occurs. The greater the substantive differences on an issue the more necessary is the application of power to settle the issue.

The power broker is one-sided in approaching the interaction between tasks and relationships. Relationships are secondary to the accomplishing of work. This is one who uses a high task and low relationship style of leadership.

Many congregations thrive under such leadership. Blue-collar churches composed of assembly-line workers are conditioned for the directive supervision this authoritarian style offers. Where churches are willing to grant highly centralized power to a minister or lay group to make the major decision for the group, this style will work. Congregations used to a more democratic tradition for decision making will not adjust to such a style.

A power broker gives maximal concern to achieving personal goals and minimal concern to relationships. Filley calls such a person a "tough battler." He says: "For such an individual, winning or losing is not merely an event; instead, he views losing as reduced status, weakness, and the loss of his self-image. On the other hand, to win gives a sense of exhilaration and achievement."[3]

The major liability of this style is that it produces overexposure of feelings, ideas, or facts without a sufficient development of trust. The power broker is one who is constantly selling himself or his ideas. He tries to motivate others to follow his leadership. If that fails, he will use manipulation to serve his goals.

The power broker possesses high levels of trust in his or her own abilities. There is little trust for others, however. This person's confidence is so strong he or she charts a direction others are expected to follow. Those who differ with this person find themselves isolated or driven from the fellowship of the congregation. Only those who are willing to be followers can work well with such an individual.

The facilitator—The fourth style of conflict minister we call the facilitator. This person is highly adaptive to a variety of situations and styles. The facilitator is one who does not function from a primary style, but shifts from style to style, depending upon the situation. The primary method of the facilitator is to seek a compromise between competing factions.

James was such a leader in the early church at Jerusalem. According to Acts 15 a deep-seated controversy arose between the Jewish believers in Jerusalem and the Gentile mission congregation in Antioch. Jewish believers accused

Paul, Barnabas, and other leaders at Antioch of teaching contrary to Jewish law. The church at Antioch believed itself consistent with the example of Jesus and the empowering of Gentiles by the Holy Spirit. Here was a fundamental issue regarding the nature of what is required to be a Christian. The atmosphere was tense; the situation could have resulted in a major schism in early Christianity. James stepped into the fray with a spirit of conciliation. He won the day by proposing a solution which could be supported by both factions. First, he appealed to Jewish tradition, the Old Testament, to support the universal application of the gospel being practiced by the Christians in Antioch (Acts 15:13-28). Second, he appealed to the leaders of the Gentile believers to insist upon a change in life-style from offensive pagan practices for Gentile converts. This compromise was accepted. Written agreements were copied to send to Gentile churches describing what had been decided. Gentiles did not have to become Jews of the flesh through circumcision to become Christians but should embody in the distinctiveness of life-style their commitment to holy living. James had facilitated an agreement which resulted in the forces of energy by the whole Christian movement upon reaching out to share its faith with the world.

Compromise is most effective as a style of ministry where the differences are attitudinal or "feeling" differences. If the conflict is rooted in substantive differences, the facilitator will be viewed with anger by all of the parties. The more the substantive issues are held with deep emotion the more difficult compromise will be; for the style calls for each side of a dispute to give up something. Conflicts rooted in emotional dysfunction will frustrate this minister because of his belief that every difference has a middle ground to which all can agree.

Highly pluralistic congregations need this style of conflict ministers within it. When a group has failed to achieve a consensus about its identity and purpose, it seeks a facilitator to keep it together. Unity will be difficult without compromise in the congregation of multiple ethnic, social class, or theological backgrounds.

Like the problem solver, the facilitator attempts to employ a balanced perspective between concern for relationships and concerns for tasks. However, he is willing to utilize any of the styles of leadership discussed in this chapter which may be necessary to conclude conflict. This adaptability and willingness to alter emphases may confuse those who tend to approach every situation in the same way.

Likewise, the facilitator balances concern for relationships with concern for personal goals. This person will attempt to achieve both, but is willing to settle for less than a maximal concern for both in order to conclude conflict more quickly.

STYLES AND RESOURCES FOR CONFLICT MINISTRY   123

The same balance between trust and exposure is maintained by the facilitator. But the intensity of each is less pronounced than for the problem solver. The facilitator has a lower level of trust in the abilities of the group, himself, or both to manage these differences.

The facilitator is willing to use power but never to the degree that major hurt will result. Power often turns to passivity in the face of major disruption. This conflict minister is constantly testing ideas, facts, and feelings with the group to ensure a power balance between factions.

The major weakness of this approach is that a group is not led far enough for consensus to emerge. The facilitator will settle for a conclusion to conflict as soon as possible with the lowest common denominator of agreement. This minister will often confuse others because of an apparent willingness to support varied positions. It appears to some that the facilitator has no inner conviction, but is a politician who will deal and trade for the quickest conclusion to an issue. Thus, the adaptability which is needed for this style weakens respect for the leader's image of integrity.

The fearful loser—The fifth style of conflict minister runs from conflict. This style is one of passivity/withdrawal. We call this person a fearful loser. Such a minister does everything possible to avoid engagement with conflict. Such persons are quiet and retiring in personal behavior. Conflict creates such intense personal insecurity the lowest risks are to be found in ignoring conflict for as long as possible. Suppression is employed to prevent conflict which often has the opposite results. Persons in suppressed conflict go underground and become behind-the-scenes combatants. The congregation is in a continual stir which others recognize, but not the fearful loser. If the underground conflict surfaces too strongly, this leader will often resign from a position of leadership or seek an opportunity for ministry elsewhere.

The leadership style of the fearful loser is one of low concern for relationships and low concern for tasks. It is a withdrawal from both relationships and work responsibilities. Others become accountable for achieving group goals. The fearful loser is equally apathetic in balancing a concern for personal goals with relationships. Such a person feels conflict is hopeless. This style "results in compliance without commitment and feelings of frustration and hostility."[3]

Passive/withdrawal persons are low trust ministers. They often have low self-images, lack personal confidence in their own abilities, and are mistrustful of others as a consequence. Conflicts cannot be engaged because there is neither trust for oneself nor the congregation to deal with it without personal hurt.

In chapter 1 we described four kinds of conflict: attitudinal, emotional, substantive, and communicative. Figure 1-1 illustrated the interrelationship between each of these. Figure 5-1 shows the relationship between various styles of conflict ministry which are described in this chapter and those kinds of

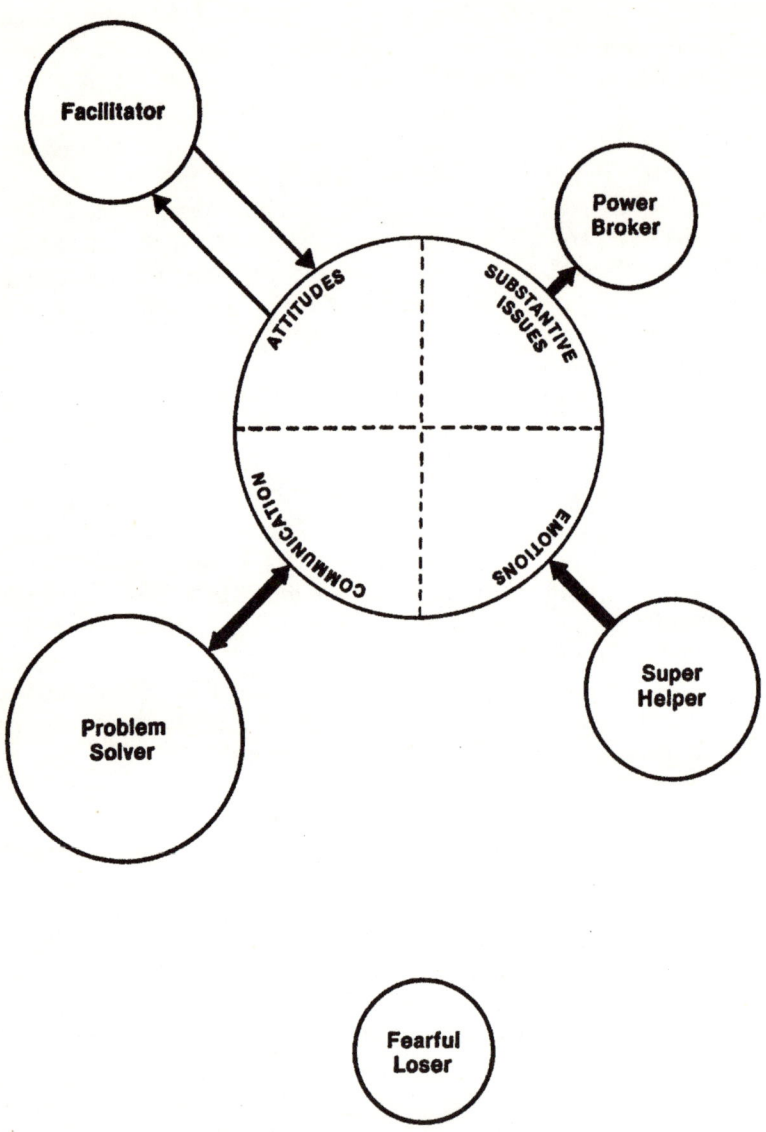

Figure 5-1: Relation Between Conflict Style and Source of Conflict

STYLES AND RESOURCES FOR CONFLICT MINISTRY 125

conflict. What we are suggesting is the nature of the conflict with which you are dealing determines the style of ministry most effective in that conflict situation.

The problem-solving style is the most preferable style to employ in conflict ministry. One ought always to attempt to minister as a problem solver. This can be done by *assuming* there is a communication problem underlying the conflict situation. The problem solver assumes attitudinal, substantive, or emotional conflict could be managed if clearer communication were brought to bear in the situation. You will note arrows denoting interaction from the communication part of Figure 5-1 to each of the other factors in conflict.

If problem solving is not possible, the second preferred style is the facilitator. Here underlying attitudes are assumed to be the root cause of the problem. Compromise between competing attitudes is attempted to settle for the best possible in the situation. The facilitator attempts maximum feedback between persons in conflict, indicating how easily he or she can be changed in the process of ministry. This is illustrated in Figure 5-1 by arrows pointing to the conflict and to the leader style. The leader is affected by conflict as much as the conflict is acted upon by the leader.

The third style one may try if neither of these is workable is that of the super helper. If deep feelings are the basis of conflict, neither of the previous styles may work. The role of the helper is supportive, rather than directive in the conflict. Dotted lines in Figure 5-1 indicate the low-risk, indirect nature of helper involvement in the conflict.

The power-broker style is appropriate when all other forms of ministry fail. The issue may be one based on substantive factors which require the most powerful to win. This style is highly directive as indicative by a heavy arrow in Figure 5-1. The power broker is subjected to few influences from the conflict itself. It is a style based upon the personal strength of the leader.

You should note in Figure 5-1 the separation of the fearful loser from kinds of conflict. This style is totally reactive, being acted upon by conflict, but not affecting it. It is the style of last resort, where all else fails. When every effort has been made without success, the only option available to the Christian leader is to withdraw from the situation.

Fortunately, many resources have been developed from a variety of sources which can be used by the contemporary conflict minister. Much can be done with these resources in diagnosis, training, and developing functional groups in the church. They are described in the remainder of this chapter as an aid in developing your skills and understanding for effective service.

Resources for Conflict Ministry

The natural question which arises from the emphases of this book is, "Where can I get help for doing a more effective job of conflict ministry?" Fortunately, there are a number of varied assessment instruments and growth resources available to assist churches in this work.

An increasing number of books in management theory, conflict management, and applications of conflict understanding to the church are available. The bibliography of this book points to those resources and will not be duplicated in this section. We will indicate other resources in this chapter which have practical value in developing healthy church life, assessing conflict potential in the church, or providing training in conflict ministry. A brief description will be given for each resource, including where it is available for purchase.

Group Development

The 1977 Annual Handbook for Group Facilitators, edited by John E. Jones and J. William Pfeiffer. University Associates, Inc., 7596 Eads Avenue, LaJolla, California 92037. This is the sixth annual edition of the most helpful resource available for group leaders. Each annual volume contains structured experiences which can be used in building groups, including conflict exercises. Sections on instrumentation, brief lectures on group development, articles on the theory of group development, and listings of resources are also included.

Assessment Tools

Career Growth Inventory by John Fabian. A helpful and simple assessment tool useful for establishing growth goals and action steps for continuing education. It provides a rating system for scaling 24 skill, attitude, and behavior areas for leaders. It is designed to elicit a self-evaluation by the leader and evaluations by five external raters. On the basis of variances between leaders and raters, as well as indicated weaknesses, the leader can project goals for continuing education to upgrade skills. It is available from Choice, Pacific Lutheran University, Tacoma, Washington 98447 at a modest cost.

Change Agent Questionnaire by Jay Hall and Martha S. Williams. Leaders in churches and community groups will profit from the use of this assessment tool. It is designed to measure one's philosophy, strategy, and evaluation of effecting change. The instrument consists of two booklets. The first is a self-scoring test in which one marks the most characteristic response to a set of change situations. Scores are then evaluated by each respondent from these questions. A variety of change agent styles can then be charted as well as the order or preference for styles. The intensity with which one uses each style is measured. One can also visualize from the instrument areas of strength and weakness for one's philosophy, strategy, and evaluation of change.

A second booklet interprets one's scores in terms of a managerial grid similar to that of the *Conflict Management Survey.* Five styles of change agentry are identified and analyzed.

This instrument can be purchased from Telometrics International, P.O. Box 314, The Woodlands, Texas 77380. It is especially helpful for church leaders engaging in community-based conflict. The instrument can be used either for training purposes or for assessing concepts of change which may be contributing to conflict within a group.

Conflict Management Survey by Jay Hall. This is a superb assessment instrument for determining one's conflict management style. It consists of two booklets. The first is an instrument on which one marks responses to a variety of conflict situations. For each situation the respondent indicates from a list of responses options of how he or she would likely deal with each situation.

A self-scoring procedure allows each person completing the instrument to determine his or her scores. The instrument allows one to assess a predominant style of conflict management, to visualize the order of styles one might use and the relative strength of each style. One can also graph scores relative to an overall personal attitude toward conflict and styles which need strengthening or weakening in how one relates to other persons, within small groups, and in intergroup settings.

A second booklet is an interpretive guide to the scores one makes on the instrument. While it can be a useful tool for individuals to analyze themselves, its best use is in the context of groups where a trained leader can guide the interpretation process. By sharing one's scores with a trusting group, confirming feedback from others can be a support of the insights revealed in the instrument.

This instrument is available from Telometrics International, P.O. Box 314, The Woodlands, Texas 77380. Many uses can be made by churches of such an instrument. It is especially valuable for church staff or leadership groups to use in analyzing their variations in approaches to conflict.

It could also be useful for persons in conflict to use to understand strategies which could be employed to work through their differences.

FIRO-B by William C. Schutz. This is a very brief, psychological measuring tool which measures six variables—expressed inclusion, wanted inclusion, expressed control, wanted control, expressed affection, and wanted affection. It is available only to educational institutions or other organizations who have trained psychologists available to administer and interpret the nature of the test. It is inexpensive and useful for illustrating some basic personality characteristics of the individuals who take it. Information regarding FIRO-B is available from Consulting Psychologist's Press, Inc., 577 College Avenue, Palo Alto, California 94306.

Leader Effectiveness and Adaptability Description (LEAD) by Paul Hersey and Kenneth H. Blanchard. An expansion of insights derived from The Leadership

Grid can be gained by using LEAD. In addition to determining one's style of leadership in terms of relationships and tasks, the intensity and adaptability of leader styles can be determined with this instrument. Thus, effectiveness of leadership style is measured. It is a useful instrument for pastors, staff leaders, and lay leaders.

The LEAD instrument, the theory upon which it is based and an interpretation of test results from it can be found in Paul Hersey and Kenneth H. Blanchard, *Management of Organizational Behavior,* Third Edition (Englewood Cliffs: Prentice-Hall, Inc., 1977), pp. 83-88, 225-272.

The Leadership Grid. A simple instrument which allows the evaluator to graph one's score on a grid measuring the relationship between concern for people and concern for production. This is a simple assessment tool which can be used by the individual and may be found on pages 140-144 in Brooks R. Faulkner, *Getting on Top of Your Work* (Nashville: Convention Press, 1973).

Management Transactions Audit by Jay Hall and C. Leo Griffith. A more general instrument for assessment purposes can be found in this tool. It's based upon the principles of Transactional Analysis and is useful for group training. Respondents score their feelings about a variety of conversations one might have with a subordinate, a colleague or a superior. After scoring one's responses a visual chart can be developed indicating whether one is responding out of a parental, adult, or child ego state. A brief interpretive manual is included with the instrument.

This resource is available from Telometrics International, P.O. Box 314, The Woodlands, Texas 77380. It is especially useful for groups who develop around the concepts of transactional analysis as a basis for group life and conversation.

Personal Relations Survey by Jay Hall and Martha S. Williams. This assessment instrument does not deal with conflict as such. However, it is useful in helping individuals understand how they relate to those with whom they work. It consists of two booklets. The first is a self-scoring test in which one indicates the most characteristic ways of responding in a variety of situations to employees, colleagues and supervisors. One then scores his or her individual responses and charts them on a Johari Window.

A second booklet interprets the meaning of the Johari Window. This is a conceptual tool which pictures how much of ourselves we reveal to others. The goal of the instrument is to help persons reveal as much of their conscious selves to others as possible within an awareness of how we are perceived by others. Healthy relationships depend upon a balancing of exposure of ourselves with a seeking of feedback from others. The booklet helps one understand the nature of personal relationships with others and to improve upon them.

The Personal Relations Survey is available from Telometrics International, P.O. Box 314, The Woodlands, Texas 77380. A filmstrip and cassette tape

STYLES AND RESOURCES FOR CONFLICT MINISTRY 129

explanation of the principles of the Johari Window are available from the same address. This resource can best be used in training programs for improving group life or working relationships among people. A church group could profit much from exploring its relational life in terms of the Johari Window as a basis for improving trust and communication within it.

16 PF Test Profile. This is a personality inventory which may be very helpful in working with individuals or assessing personality factors for church staff members. It is a detailed psychological testing instrument which measures 16 basic personality characteristics helpful for understanding and interpreting one's style of management and relationship with people. It is a tool which should be used by a trained counselor. Many business firms and educational institutions use the instrument to assess variables indicative of leadership ability. One of the factors measured is tension which can be useful in working with overstressed persons.

The 16 PF Test Profile is available through the Institute for Personality and Ability Testing, 1602-04 Coronado Drive, Champaign, Illinois 61820 and through licensed psychologists or college and university departments of psychology.

What Are the Priorities? By Lyle E. Schaller. This is a useful group discussion starter which can be used by pastoral search committees or pastoral evaluation committees to develop consensus regarding clergy role priorities. It is 12 cards with specific roles described on each. After each group member stacks the cards according to his or her priorities, the group discusses the differences or similarities of expectations which emerge.

The use of this exercise is describe in Lyle E. Schaller, *The Pastor and the People* (Nashville: Abingdon Press, 1973), pp. 45-55.

Simulation Games and Programmed Learning Resources

Agenda: A Simulation of Decision Making in a Church Assembly by John C. Bryan, Rudolph W. Graham, and Richard M. Slyman. This simulation game provides a learning experience in understanding the conflicts of interests and complexity of a church denominational body. It offers opportunities for players to negotiate, confront, strategize, speak, and engage in parliamentary procedure. An awareness of church structures and the decision-making process emerges from playing the game. It is useful for church groups in training for handling organizational conflict. Two to six hours of playing and debriefing time are needed. This simulation is available from John Knox Press, Box 1176, Richmond, Virginia.

Church Conflict: Crisis or Challenge by Cecil E. Marsh. A very simple and usable multimedia kit for study groups can be found in this resource. The kit contains a programmed learning package of four sessions for five persons.

Each contains a booklet describing conflict biblically and practically. Structured group activities including worksheets, a filmstrip, and cassette recording complete the kit. It is available from The Sunday School Board of the Southern Baptist Convention, 127 Ninth Avenue, North, Nashville, Tennessee 37234.

The Loveable Church Game: An Experience of Congregational Conflict by Theodore D. Peck. The realities of power within a contemporary congregation are experienced in this game. Competing expectations of various roles such as black-white, male-female, rich-poor, and mission-antimission groups are simulated. Conflict is the usual result of the game. It is available from the Westminster Press, Witherspoon Building, Philadelphia, Pennsylvania 19107.

Starpower by R. Garry Shirts. An explosive situation of conflict can be created by this dynamic power game. It is simple and can be played quickly. Two hours of playing time will give to a group its benefits. The players trade chips and are rewarded for success. The result is three groups based upon wealth represented by chips. The wealthy are able to become wealthier while controlling the outcome of the game. The poor become poorer and usually angrier until the game ends. It is available from Western Behavioral Sciences Institute, 1150 Silverado, LaJolla, California.

Witherspoon Church: A Simulation of Decision-Making in a Local Church by William R. Knox and Gus Root. Local church leaders will find this simulation game helpful in training for decision making, planning and budgeting. Decisions at a congregational level are made demanding an evaluation of functioning. The game requires six hours of playing time. It may be ordered from John Knox Press, Box 1176, Richmond, Virginia.

Notes

[1] Keith Nickle, The Collection: *A Study in Paul's Strategy,* Studies in Biblical Theology, Vol. 48 (Napierville, Ill.: Alex R. Allenson, Inc., 1966).

[2] The styles in this chapter have been adapted with considerable variation from the Conflict Management Survey. See Jay Hall, *How to Interpret Your Scores from the Conflict Management Survey* (The Wooldlands, Texas: Telometrics International, 1973) for a management approach to conflict.

[3] Alan L. Filley, *Interpersonal Conflict Resolution* (Glenview, Ill.: Scott, Foresman and Co., 1975), p. 51.

STYLES AND RESOURCES FOR CONFLICT MINISTRY

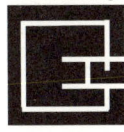

The Continuing Education Unit •

Assignment

1. The authors identify five styles of managing conflict.
   (a) Describe the strengths and weaknesses of each style.
   (b) Evaluate your style and determine your "primary" and "secondary" or back-up style.
   (c) What do you need to change in order to be more effective as a conflict minister.

2. Select one of the "Assessment Tools" listed on pages. 126-129 that will enable you to accurately determine your conflict management style.

Conclusions
Will Conflict Never End?

As we set forth our goals for this book in the preface we focused most of our attention upon the human communities which must learn how to practice conflict ministry. We were tempted many times to state ideals, even to preach concerning what ought to be. In the previous chapters we have resisted that temptation in order to give attention to pragmatic realities. Our concern was to assist others to *do* conflict ministry more effectively. So we promised to focus upon churches as sociological communities of hope rather than the church as a theological community of promise.

Such distinctions do not maintain themselves so easily. As real people practice the gifts of grace, they become the gifts of grace. As churches work at the tasks of applying the truths of faith, they become the community of faith. For where there is genuine being there shall be activity which grows out of being. Second Peter 1:3-11 describes the circle of the Christian life as a dynamic interaction between believing, growing, and doing. Through knowledge of Christ every provision has been made for life as a promise from God. The action of faith produces virtue, knowledge, self-control, steadfastness, godliness, brotherly affection, and love. Each of these contributes to growth in the knowledge of Christ which is the beginning of faith.

That process of growth summarizes the nature of conflict ministry. One begins in the risks of trust toward others and exposure of feelings, attitudes, and facts. As growth occurs action takes place. The arena of risk is expanded to even larger areas of life so the more one serves as a reconciler in Christ, the more reconciling ministry there is to do.

Such an ever-expanding circle of need could be cause for despair. "Why keep trying," you say, "when there will never be an end to conflict?" It is at that point the resources of Christian faith must be brought to bear upon our understandings.

We began this journey with you emphasizing the theological aspects of conflict. It is there we must conclude, for hope is rested in God. Our hope that reconciliation is Gods's way, that there is ministry in engaging conflict, and that there is a final end to conflict is a by-product of faith. We keep on working as conflict ministers of reconciliation because we believe in God's good time reconciliation will be the order of reality, rather than conflict. So, as we began trying to understand conflict in relation to God, we must conclude similarly. We have drawn from many sources in the development of these guidelines—biblical examples, cases of contemporary church situations, management theory, and social psychological analyses. Overarching each of these has been an effort to develop an integrated approach consistent with the insights of the Christian faith. So it is that we conclude with hope rooted in Jesus Christ.

The first implication of these Christian beliefs is that the disciples of Jesus Christ accept the reality of conflict which belongs to every aspect of life. The world in which we live is not an idyllic paradise and never will be apart from the grace of God. To say that man is fallen is to say that conflict invades every dimension of human experience. There are not persons who do not wrestle, as the apostle Paul, with the difficulties of right action:

> For I know that nothing good dwells within me, that is, in my flesh. I can will what is right, but I cannot do it. For I do not do the good I want, but the evil I do not want is what I do. Now if I do what I do not want, it is no longer I that do it, but sin which dwells within me (Rom. 7:18-20).

There are no human institutions which do not participate in sin, hence conflict. Every government, every marriage, every economy, every school, every church lives with the daily struggles of life east of Eden in the land of Nod.

The impact of sin has made its mark upon every aspect of humanity and none can escape it. This is surely the meaning of the Pauline declaration, "None is righteous, no, not one" (Rom. 3:9) and the Johannine admonition, "If we say we have no sin, we deceive ourselves, and the truth is not in us" (1 John 1:8). Truth and righteousness can be experienced in human community in spite of the universality of sin through the presence of God in our lives and our world.

Most Christians have little difficulty in accepting this traditional theology until it is applied to the Christian community. We grant fallibility to every agency of life except one. That is the church. In our experience it is often the very people who speak most vociferously of the impact of human sin in our world who expect a kind of sinless perfection of what is an institution of sinners.

That is what a church is. It is a body of people who claim obedience to the lordship of Jesus Christ. Thus, it is a group of sinners who have come to the recognition of their need for reconciliation with God. It is a fellowship of sinners who are forgiven and free to live according to God's will. It will not do so in every case, but can be used of God in spite of such imperfection. It is a fellowship which lives with the ambiguity of constantly choosing sin, but trusting in the forgiveness of God for that sin. It is a pilgrimage of persons seeking the better way of the Father and finding it as a struggle with principalities and powers. It is a treasure in an earthen vessel—the treasure is the presence of the spirit of Christ within its human form.[1]

No church will every successfully manage the conflicts which are inevitable within every human reality until it is able to accept the fact that it is a human vessel. This is perhaps the most difficult step in the process of a healthy congregational life. The admission must constantly be made by God's people, "We have problems among us. We are not perfect. Let us work together to seek the reconciling Spirit of Christ so that we may be one."

There is a second implication of a theological understanding of conflict. Reconciliation cannot be achieved without conflicts.[2] The word comes from the Greek word *katallasso* which means "to change, to exchange, to reconcile." [3] The process of changing cannot occur unless there is the need for change, a dissatisfaction with things as they are. The most profound biblical passages about reconciliation are found in the Pauline letters. In every instance there is a call for reconciliation amid conflict. Humanity and God are in conflict. Enmity (i.e., hatred or hostility) is the product of their separateness. God's initiative in facing the conflict through the suffering love of His Son's death on the cross bridges that separation. Jews and Gentiles, male and female, slaves and free are in conflict with each other. Because God's example is universal, the recipients of His love must follow it by taking initiative toward those with whom they experience conflict to bridge their differences (Gal. 3:28).

Reconciliation among the factions of the human family is not simply a high ideal. It requires the difficulty of face-to-face struggle with the issues that separate people from each other and a commitment to living with the cross of suffering to effect change. Change seldom occurs without conflict. Reconciliation is a process of change. It forces to the surface of consciousness attitudes, behaviors, and emotions that are often volatile. It can heal them. That is the good news of the gospel.

There is a final implication of the Christian faith for handling conflict. Thus far the words have been discouraging ones for they call for demanding struggle. The only way we can live with the realism of human fallibility and the costs of reconciliation is that we have a hopeful vision of the promises of God. We can act righteously now because we are committed to God's promise of a future eternity. All of the costs of reconciliation are worth it because God promises eternal reward to those who are faithful to His call. How is it that the Christian can engage the forces of conflict in a fallen world without despair? Because of the vision of what is to come! A faith that is not futuristic is a faith that cannot survive the struggle of handling conflict. The promise of the future coming of Jesus as King is the vision of a redeemed cosmos where the harmony of creation will be restored, where persons will live in a reconciled community and where peace settles the conflicts of life. "Will conflict never end?" Yes, when God's kingdom comes on earth to bring eternal life.

To live the vision of the end, according to Jesus, is to live the vision now. That is why we must affirm our own hope in this book. The trust that underlies it is the faith that congregations who struggle to embody the vision of the kingdom by dealing forthrightly with the conflicts they encounter may experience together the fruits of the promise which God gives—reconciliation in the midst of community.

Maranatha. Lord Jesus come!

Notes

[1] James Gustafson, *Treasure in Earthen Vessels: The Church as a Human Community* (New York: Harper, 1961) ascribes the uniqueness of the church to its confession of Jesus as Lord. It shares with other institutions likeness as a natural community, a political community, a community of language, a community of interpretation, a community of memory and understanding, and a community of belief and action.

[2] This idea is also developed in a different way in Paul A. Mickey and Robert L. Wilson, *Conflict and Resolution* (Nashville: Abingdon Press, 1973), pp. 13-22.

[3] Friedrich Büchsel, "katallasso," *A Theological Dictionary of the New Testament*, I, ed. by Gerhard Kittel, trans. and ed. by Geoffrey W. Bromiley (Grand Rapids: Wm. B. Eerdmans Publishing Co., 1964), pp. 254-258.

Bibliography

Books

Anderson, James D. and Ezra Earl Jones. *The Management of Ministry.* New York: Harper and Row, 1978.

Appley, Mortimer and Richard Trumball (eds.) *Psychological Stress: Issues in Research.* New York: Appleton-Century-Crofts, 1967.

Augsberger, David W. *Caring Enough to Confront.* Glendale, CA: Regal Books, 1973.

Bach, George R. and Peter Wyden. *The Intimate Enemy: How to Fight Fair in Love and Marriage.* Caldwell, NJ: Morrow, 1969.

Bailey, Derrick Sherwin. *The Mystery of Love and Marriage.* New York: Harper and Bros. Publishing Co., 1952.

Bellah, Robert. *Beyond Belief: Essays on Religion in a Post-Traditional World.* New York: Harper and Row, 1970.

Benson, Herbert. *The Relaxation Response.* Caldwell, NJ: William Morrow and Co., 1975.

Berne, Eric. *Games People Play: The Psychology of Human Relationships.* New York: Grove Press, 1967.

Biersdorf, John E. *Hunger for Experience in Vital Religious Communities in America Today.* New York: Seabury Press, 1976.

——— (ed.). *Creating an Intentional Ministry.* Nashville: Abingdon Press, 1976.

Broadbert, Donald Eric. *Decision and Stress.* New York: Academic Press, 1971.

Brown, Barbara B. *New Mind, New Body, Biofeedback: New Directions for the Mind.* New York: Harper and Row, 1974.

———. *Stress and the Art of Biofeedback.* New York: Harper and Row, 1976.

Bry, Adelaide. *EST: 60 Hours that Transform Your Life.* New York: Harper and Row, 1976.

Carson, Daniel H. and B. L. Driver. *An Ecological Approach to Environmental Stress.* Ann Arbor: Mental Health Research Institute, University of Michigan, 1966.

Collins, Randall. *Conflict Sociology: Toward and Explanatory Science.* New York: Academic Press, 1975.

Coelho, George C., David Hamburg and John E. Adams. *Coping and Adaptation.* New York: Basic Books, 1974.

Deutsch, Morton. *The Resolution of Conflict: Constructive and Destructive Processes.* New Haven: Yale University Press, 1973.

Dittes, James E. *When the People Say No: Conflict and the Call to Ministry.* San Francisco: Harper and Row, 1979.

Dohrenwend, Barbara Snell and Bruce P. *Conference on Stressful Life Events: Their Nature and Effects.* New York: Wiley, 1974.

Ellul, Jacques. *The Ethics of Freedom.* Trans. and ed. by Geoffrey W. Bromiley. Grand Rapids: Wm. B. Eerdmans Publishing Co., 1976.

———. *The Meaning of the City.* Trans. by Dennis Pardee. Grand Rapids: Wm. B. Eerdmans Publishing Co., 1970.

Filley, Alan. *Interpersonal Conflict Resolution.* Glenview, Ill.: Scott, Foresman and Co., 1975.

Frederick, Carl, *est: Playing the Game* the New Way, *The Game of Life.* New York: Del Publishing Co., 1974.

Funkenstein, Daniel H., Stanley H. King and Margaret E. Drolette. *Mastery of Stress.* Cambridge: Harvard University Press, 1957.

Glass, David C. and Jerome E. Singer. *Urban Stress: Experiments on Noise and Social Stressors.* New York: Academic Press, 1972.

Greer, Scott. *The Emerging City: Myth and Reality.* New York: Free Press of Glencoe, 1962.

Gross, Nancy E. *Living with Stress.* New York: McGraw-Hill, 1958.

Gustafson, James. *Treasure in Earthen Vessels: The Church as a Human Community.* New York: Harper and Row, 1961.

Hadden, Jeffrey K. *The Gathering Storm in the Churches: A Sociologist's View of the Widening Gap Between Clergy and Laymen.* New York: Doubleday, 1969.

——— and Charles F. Longino, Jr. *Gideon's Gang: A Case Study of the Church in Social Action.* Philadelphia: Pilgrim Press, 1974.

Harkness, Georgia. *The Ministry of Reconciliation.* Nashville: Abingdon Press, 1971.

Harris, Douglas James. *Shalom: The Biblical Concept of Peace.* Grand Rapids: Baker Book House, 1970.

Harris, Thomas A. *I'm OK—You're OK: A Practical Guide to Transactional Analysis.* New York: Harper and Row, 1969.

Hoge, Dean R. *Division in the Protestant House.* Philadelphia: The Westminster Press, 1976.

James, Muriel. *Born to Love: Transactional Analysis in the Church.* Reading, Mass.: Addison-Wesley Publishing Co., 1973.

Jones, Ezra Earl and Robert L. Wilson. *What's Ahead for Old First Church*. New York: Harper & Row, 1974.
Jud, Gerald J., Edgar W. Mills, Jr. and Genevieve Burch. *Ex-Pastors: Why Men Leave the Parish Ministry*. Philadelphia: Pilgrim Press, 1970.
Kelley, Dean M. *Why Conservative Churches Are Growing*. New York: Harper and Row, 1971.
Lazarus, Richard S. *Psychological Stress and the Coping Process*. New York: McGraw-Hill, 1966.
Leas, Speed and Paul Kittlaus. *Church Fights: Managing Conflict in the Local Church*. Philadelphia: The Westminster Press, 1973.
Lee, Dallas. *The Cotton Patch Evidence*. New York: Harper and Row, 1971.
Levi, Lennart. *Stress: Sources, Management and Prevention, Medical and Psychological Aspects of the Stress of Everyday Life*. Trans. by Patrick Hort. New York: Liveright Publishing Corp., 1967.
Levine, Sol. and Norman A. Scotch (ed.). *Social Stress*. Chicago: Aldine Pub. Co., 1970.
Levinson, Daniel J., et al. *The Seasons of a Man's Life*. New York: Alfred A. Knopf, 1978.
Likert, Rensis and Jane Gibson. *New Ways of Managing Conflict*. New York: McGraw-Hill Book Co., 1976.
Lindaman, Edward B. *Thinking in the Future Tense*. Nashville: Broadman Press, 1978.
Luce, Gay Gaer. *Body Time: Physiological Rhythms and Social Stress*. New York: Random House, 1971.
McGrath, Joseph E. (ed.). *Social and Psychological Factors in Stress*. New York: Holt, Rinehart and Winston, 1970.
Maston, T. B. *Why Live the Christian Life?* Nashville: Thomas Nelson, Inc., 1974.
Mickey, Paul A. and Robert L. Wilson. *Conflict and Resolution*. Nashville: Abingdon Press, 1973.
Mickey, Paul Gamble and Paula Gilbert. *Pastoral Assertiveness: A New Model for Pastoral Care*. Nashville: Abingdon, 1978.
Miller, John M. *The Contentious Community: Constructive Conflict in the Church*. Philadelphia: The Westminster Press, 1978.
Mills, Edgar W. and John P. Koval. *Stress in the Ministry*. New York: IDOC, 1971.
Moltmann, Jürgen. *The Crucified God: The Cross of Christ as the Foundation and Criticism of Christian Theology*. New York: Harper and Row, 1974.
———. *The Theology of Hope*. London: SCM Press, 1967.
Nickle, Keith. *The Collection: A Study in Paul's Strategy,* Studies in Biblical Theology, vol. 48, Naperville, Ill.: Alex R. Allenson, Inc., 1966.

Nouwen, Henri. *The Wounded Healer.* Garden City, NY: Doubleday & Co., Inc., 1972.

Oates, Wayne E. *Pastoral Counseling.* Philadelphia: Westminster Press, 1974.

Packard, Vance. *A Nation of Strangers.* New York: David McKay Company, Inc., 1972.

Perls, Frederick S., Ralph F. Hefferline and Paul Goodman. *Gestalt Therapy: Excitement and Growth in the Human Personality.* New York: Dell Publishing Co., 1951.

Quinley, Harold E. *The Prophetic Clergy: Social Activism Among Protestant Clergy.* New York: John Wiley & Sons, 1974.

Robinson, John A. T. *The Human Face of God.* Philadelphia: The Westminster Press, 1973.

Rust, E. Warren (compiler). *The Mobile American and Multifamily Housing.* Atlanta: Home Mission Board, S.B.C., 1976.

Savage, John S. *The Apathetic and Bored Church Member.* Pittsford, NY: LEAD Consultants, 1976.

Schaller, Lyle E. *Assimilating New Members,* Creative Leadership Series, ed. by Lyle E. Schaller. Nashville: Abingdon Press, 1978.

———.*The Change Agent.* Nashville: Abingdon Press, 1972.

———. *Hey, That's Our Church!* Nashville: Abingdon Press, 1975.

———. *Parish Planning: How to Get Things Done in Your Church.* Nashville: Abingdon Press, 1971.

———. *The Pastor and the People: Building a New Partnership for Effective Ministry.* Nashville: Abingdon Press, 1973.

———. *Survival Tactics in the Parish.* Nashville: Abingdon Press, 1977.

Schmidt, Paul F. *Coping with Difficult People,* ed. Wayne E. Oates. Philadelphia: The Westminster Press, 1980.

Selye, Hans. *Stress Without Distress.* Philadelphia: Lippincott, 1974.

———. *The Stress of Life.* New York: McGraw-Hill Book Company, Inc., 1956.

Shriver, Donald W., Jr. and Karl A Ostrum. *Is There Hope for the City?* Philadelphia: The Westminster Press, 1977.

Specter, Gerald A. and William L. Clairborn (eds.). *Crisis Intervention.* New York: Behavioral Publications, 1973.

Stagner, Ross (compiler). *The Dimensions of Human Conflict.* Detroit: Wayne State University Press, 1967.

Stotts, Jack L. *Shalom: The Search for a Peaceable City.* Nashville: Abingdon Press, 1973.

Walton, Richard E. *Interpersonal Peacemaking: Confrontations and Third Party Consultation.* Reading, Massachusetts: Addison-Wesley Publishing Company, Inc. 1969.

Winter, J. Alan. *Continuities in the Sociology of Religion: Creed, Congregation, and Community.* New York: Harper and Row, Inc., 1977.

Wuthnow, Robert. *The Consciousness Reformation.* Berkeley: University of California Press, 1976.

Articles

"A Moving Story—Is It True," *San Francisco Sunday Examiner and Chronicle,* November 7, 1976, p. 6.

Büchsel, Friedrich. "Katallasso," *A Theological Dictionary of the New Testament* I. Ed. by Gerhard Kittel, trans. by and ed. by Geoffrey W. Bromiley. Grand Rapids: Wm. B. Eerdmans Publishing Co., 1964.

Coleman, James S. "Social Cleavage and Religious Conflict," *The Journal of Social Issues,* XII:44-56, 1956.

Dittes, James E., "To Accept and Celebrate Conflict," *Ministry Studies,* II (December, 1968), 43-46.

Foerster, Werner, "eirene," *Theological Dictionary of the New Testament,* II. Ed. by Gerhard Kittel, trans. by Geoffrey W. Bromiley. Grand Rapids: Wm. B. Eerdmans Publishing Co., 1964.

Heinz, Donald. "The Christian World Liberation Front," *The New Religious Consciousness.* Ed. by Charles Y. Glock and Robert N. Bellah. Berkeley: University of California Press, 1976.

Holmes, Thomas H. and Richard H. Rahe. "The Social Readjustment Rating Scale," *Journal of Psychosomatic Research* 11 (2): 213-218, 1967.

Jarvis, Peter, "The Ministry-Laity Relationship: A Case of Potential Conflict," *Sociological Analysis,* 37:74-80, 1976.

Johnson, Sherman E. "Matthew," *The Interpreter's Bible,* VII. Ed. by George Arthur Buttrick. New York: Abingdon Press, 1951.

Jones, John E. and Anthony G. Banet, Jr. "Dealing with Anger," *The 1976 Handbook for Group Facilitators.* Ed. by J. William Pfeiffer and John E. Jones. LaJolla, CA: University Associates, Inc., 1976, pp. 111-113.

Kemper, Robert G. "Small Issues and Massive Revelation," *Creating an Intentional Ministry.* Ed. by John Biersdorf. Nashville: Abingdon Press, 1976.

Kelly, James R. "Escaping the Dilemma: Reconciliation and a Communication Model of Conflict," *Review of Religious Research* 19:167-177, Winter 1978.

Lally, John Jr. "A Theology of Conflict," *Commonwealth,* LXXXVI:355-358, December 15, 1967.

McGrath, Joseph E. "Settings, Measures, and Themes: An Integrative Review of Some Research on Social-Psychological Factors in Stress," in *Social and Psychological Factors in Stress.* Ed. by Joseph E. McGrath. New York: Holt, Rinehart and Winston, 1970, pp. 58-96.

Meadows, Paul, "Models, Systems and Science," *American Sociological Review,* 22:3-9, February, 1957.

Stein, Ruth, "Stresses That Hurt the Most," *San Francisco Chronicle,* November 9, 1976, p. 18.

Stone, Donald. "The Human Potential Movement," *The New Religious Consciousness.* Ed. by Charles Y. Glock and Robert N. Bellah. Berkeley: University of California Press, 1976.

Wallace, Robert K. and Herbert Benson, "The Physiology of Meditation," *Scientific American,* 226: (1972).

Westhues, Kenneth. "The Church in Opposition," *Sociological Analysis,* 37:299-314, 1976.

Yeats, William Butler. "The Second Coming," *Selected Poems and Two Plays of William Butler Yeats.* Ed. by M. L. Rosenthal, New York: Collier Books, 1962.

CEU Registration Request

MCM 7566
Conflict Ministry in the Church

This is to certify that I have read this volume and completed all the readings and exercises assigned at the end of each chapter. I have spent a total of twenty hours or more with these assignments and I hereby apply for two Continuing Education Units.*

Name _____

Address _____

_____

Date _____ Social Security/ID No. _____

Signature _____

EVALUATION

Please answer three questions:

1. What was the greatest strength of this reading exercise?

2. What was its major weakness?

3. How do you plan to use in your ministry what you have learned?

Instructions:
   To Participants: Send this form to your ministerial secretary for recording your CEUs.
   To Ministerial Secretaries: When the CEUs have been applied to the participant's Service Record, please send this form to your Division Center of Continuing Education for Ministers.
   *CEUs are non-academic credit and cannot be applied to a degree.